Mother of Courage

The True Story of an Armless Dentist and Her Triumph Over Tragedy

By

Dr. Philip Chanin

and Bill Snyder

DORRANCE PUBLISHING CO
EST. 1920
PITTSBURGH, PENNSYLVANIA 15238

The contents of this work, including, but not limited to, the accuracy of events, people, and places depicted; opinions expressed; permission to use previously published materials included; and any advice given or actions advocated are solely the responsibility of the author, who assumes all liability for said work and indemnifies the publisher against any claims stemming from publication of the work.

All Rights Reserved
Copyright © 2024 by Dr. Philip Chanin

No part of this book may be reproduced or transmitted, downloaded, distributed, reverse engineered, or stored in or introduced into any information storage and retrieval system, in any form or by any means, including photocopying and recording, whether electronic or mechanical, now known or hereinafter invented without permission in writing from the publisher.

Dorrance Publishing Co
585 Alpha Drive
Pittsburgh, PA 15238
Visit our website at www.dorrancebookstore.com

ISBN: 979-8-88925-499-7
eISBN: 979-8-88925-506-2

TABLE OF CONTENTS

Chapter One
The Accident 1

Chapter Two
Learning to Swim Again 11

Chapter Three
Now It Is Up to You 20

Chapter Four
Freedom from Fear 27

Chapter Five
Red Pencil 35

Chapter Six
Lessons in Courage 47

Chapter Seven
City of Angels, City of Hope 57

Chapter Eight
A Rare Case 65

Chapter Nine
The Best Driver 74

Chapter Ten
Dark Father 82

Chapter Eleven
A Special Burden 93

Chapter Twelve
The Salt Wagon Story 100

Chapter Thirteen
Open a Door 112

Chapter Fourteen
Such a Time as This 120

Chapter Fifteen
There Must Be a Dawn 128

Chapter Sixteen
Hand in Cap 137

Chapter Seventeen
An Answered Prayer 145

Chapter Eighteen
How to Survive a Bear Attack 155

Chapter Nineteen
Knowledge is the Key 165

Chapter Twenty
A Path with Heart 172

Epilogue 180

Acknowledgments 188

Chapter One
The Accident

On June 29, 1941, the last Sunday of the month, 24-year-old Margaret Jones of Osceola, Arkansas, was sailing with friends on the San Jacinto River that flows through Houston, Texas, into the Gulf of Mexico, when her world was blown apart.

Margaret Jones' college portrait

Margaret was one of two female students at the Texas Dental College in Houston. She'd completed her second year of studies and two weeks earlier had taken the state board entrance exams for her junior year. The poised and strikingly attractive blue-eyed blonde made friends easily, but she was equally ambitious and fiercely independent. She paid her own way. As assistant to the head of the Department of Bacteriology, she taught freshman courses and maintained the laboratory's drug stock. Margaret knew who she was and where she was going.

The May Ellen was an 18-foot sloop, a sailboat with a mainsail port and smaller headsail aft secured to a 28-foot mast with metal rigging. Ellen Wellensiek, the boat's owner, was the other female student at the college, a rising senior. As the dock was just 20 miles east of campus, the two women frequently spent their Sunday afternoons out on the water with male companions.

On this balmy Sunday afternoon, Ellen had invited along her brother-in-law, Robert Way Schlumpf, chief metallurgist at the Hughes Tool Company in Houston. The company's founder, Howard Hughes Sr., patented the two-cone rotary drill bit that revolutionized oil well drilling during the early years of the Texas Oil Boom. Hughes' son, also named Howard, was the famous pilot and business tycoon.

Margaret's date was Louis W. "Lou" Lynch, 25, a senior at the dental college from California whom she'd met at a dance the previous November. A dashing young man with a mustache, big smile, and eyes that twinkled mischievously behind wire-rimmed glasses, Lou was her "steady." As he was leaving that night to spend the summer at his home in San Francisco, the boating party dropped off his trunk at the railroad station on the way to the harbor.

Margaret and Lou at a college function in early 1941

Joining them on the outing that day was the dean of the college, Frederick C. Elliott, DDS, who was in the middle of engineering the small college's affiliation with the University of Texas system to ensure its long-term survival. Elliott, an avid boater himself, made it a point to get to know and socialize with as many of the 100-odd students in the four-year college as he could. From the two-man dinghy he and another student were rowing alongside the sailboat, the dean suggested that the party head for a sandy cove in Old River Bay to swim.

The place seemed ideal, a shallow tidewater end of the bay just off the west approach of the Market Street truss bridge that spanned the San Jacinto River. The water was about five feet deep, and the cove had a smooth, sandy bottom. Parallel to the bridge a high-voltage power line stretched across the river, supported by a series of poles.

After an afternoon of swimming and playing and "cuttin' up," around 5 p.m. the party decided to head for home. As the surface of the water reflected a rosy glow from the setting sun, Ellen and Robert hoisted the sails while Margaret and Lou pulled the boat into deeper water. Margaret felt something pinch her leg. Lou was standing in the shallow water behind her. "It's shrimp biting," he joked. To escape his teasing, Margaret grabbed the anchor chain and threw her feet against the prow of the boat. Lou put his hands on her arms to steady her.

At that instant, the mast of the boat, which had been drifting across the bay, contacted a sagging portion of the power line that was virtually indistinguishable from the bridge in the sunset. Like a lightning bolt, a surge of 12,000 volts of electricity crackled down the metal rigging, through the anchor chain and into Margaret's arms. The current was so intense it welded the chain links together. Passing through her arms into Lou's body, the current found grounding in the bottom of the bay. Lou was killed instantly. Electrocuted. The current continued to hiss and pop until, with all her might, Ellen swung a wooden paddle against the mast to break the connection. Unconscious, Margaret dropped from the boat and sank beneath the water.

Robert jumped into the water, pulled Margaret out, and brought her back onto the boat. Ellen, a former camp counselor who knew how to perform artificial respiration, repeatedly pressed Margaret's chest until she coughed and started breathing again. Robert returned to the water, and with the help of a young man who'd witnessed the accident from shore, located Lou's body after a few minutes. By then, rescuers from the Tri-Cities First Aid Unit had arrived with oxygen tanks. For more than two hours, they administered resuscitation but could not revive the young man. After a justice of the peace determined the cause of death, his body was taken to a nearby funeral home until his family in

California could be contacted and arrangements could be made.

Margaret vaguely remembered being "dragged" into a sheriff's car, rushed to a nearby hospital, given emergency treatment, and transported later that night to Houston's Baptist Memorial Hospital, which had a burn specialist. At some point during the transport, she regained partial consciousness and groggily told her rescuers, "I've been sunburned before. I can take it."

She was never fully conscious. The pain of her injuries was so excruciating that she was given heavy doses of morphine to knock her out. From the time she was admitted, her doctors were certain that they would have to amputate her arms. But the burn specialist advised them to wait until there was a "clear demarcation" between damaged and healthy tissue. "If we amputate tonight, we'll probably have to amputate again, and she'll never survive two surgeries," he told them.

Reached by telephone, Margaret's parents, Mae and Robert Haskin Jones, borrowed money for two train fares and a friend rushed them by car to Memphis in time to catch the 10 p.m. train. By the time they arrived in Houston at 2 p.m. the next afternoon, her condition was deteriorating. The high voltage that had welded together the metal links of the anchor chain had burned away half of the palms of her hands and destroyed the muscle tissue and vasculature of her arms.

Doctors couldn't stop the bleeding. Repeated blood transfusions were required. The hospital sent out a desperate call to the dental college for blood donors. Several students responded, trooping to the hospital to see if their blood type matched Margaret's, volunteering to help to save her life.

Mae sat vigil at her daughter's bedside day and night, tears flowing freely, at times convulsed by sobs. It was as if her heart was being ripped out of her chest. And yet amidst the horror and pain she was experiencing, she did not give into despair.

Her sweet girl was alive. God had a plan for her. Even from this cruel, disfiguring catastrophe, God's Will would triumph somehow. Mae was as certain of this as she had been of anything in her life.

For there was something special about Margaret Ethel Jones, Mae's second child, the youngest of three children in the family. Margaret was born on June 2, 1917, in the log farmhouse her father had built 21 years earlier at Carson

Lake, a farming village in rural northeast Arkansas, about 12 miles south of the Mississippi River town of Osceola.

At the time Robert Haskin Jones, who usually went by his nickname, "Haskins," managed a 2,000-acre parcel of a nearby plantation, Nodena. The fields of Nodena yielded mainly corn, hay, and cotton, but the plantation was best known for its ancient burial sites.

Because neighbors were few and far between, as a youngster Margaret played with the children of the Black laborers who worked the land. They lived in the cabins by the barns and blacksmith shop. She'd pull her playmates in her little red wagon, bandage their cuts, and slip food to them from the kitchen when her mother wasn't looking.

In early 20th century Arkansas, as was the case throughout the South, segregation was the law of the land. Yet Margaret was only emulating her mother. Mae, a former schoolteacher who recently had begun writing for the local newspaper, didn't let anyone tell her how to live. She marched as a suffragette for the right of women to vote. When the Blacks who lived on the plantation were ill or injured, she brought home remedies to their cabins. That was how she lived her faith. For many years, Mae taught Sunday School and Haskins served as a deacon at their local church. But they believed the path to their true calling lay beyond the chapel walls.

Mae Jones in her later years

In 1928 Haskins left the plantation for the oil business—he sold fuel to local farmers. But when the market crashed in 1929, plunging the world into the Great Depression, the farmers couldn't pay what they owed, and Haskins lost the business. To make ends meet, Mae rented a hotel in Osceola and became its proprietress, while Haskins signed on as the town's night marshal. But the hotel failed, and in 1933, the family had to move in with relatives in the country.

Margaret had completed ninth grade in town, but her parents couldn't afford to pay for room and board so she could return to her high school in the fall. Sure enough, ever-plucky Margaret found a way. She had befriended a woman from Chicago who had stayed at her mother's hotel and who was searching for daughters she'd lost in a divorce. When Margaret tracked them down through the papers to a Memphis address, the grateful woman invited her to return with her to Chicago and finish high school there. Margaret declined the charity but said she'd come if she could work for her room and board.

In September 1933, 16-year-old Margaret found herself on a train bound for Chicago. Her parents barely scraped up the money for the fare. Among her mother's parting gifts was a Bible. Tucked into the fly leaves were several inspirational messages clipped from the newspaper that, as Margaret noted years later in one of her scrapbooks, were "Mother's effort to guide me."

One of the sayings, "The soul is dyed the color of its thoughts," goes back to the ancient Greek philosopher Heraclitus. It continues: "Think only on those things that are in line with your principles and can bear the light of day. The content of your character is your choice. Day by day, what you do is what you become. Your integrity is your destiny—it is the light that guides your way."

In Chicago, Margaret enrolled as a junior in the prestigious Nicholas Senn High School, named for the famed military surgeon. The woman she'd befriended had found her a job working for a woman with two young children. Margaret cleaned house, and every morning before walking two miles to school, fired up the furnace in the basement. The work was onerous and the experience a miserable one, but although she was lonely and scared, in her letters home Margaret exuded sweetness and wide-eyed curiosity.

In her 1934 Mother's Day letter, she wrote: "Never do I wake in the morning or go to sleep at night that I do not think of the best Mother and Daddy that a girl could have." Later in the letter, she described the dust storm that swept up from the Great Plains on May 10, blotting out the sun and dumping 12 million pounds of dirt onto the city of Chicago. "I cleaned the whole house yesterday," she continued. "I was so tired I didn't dust my room and it's about to wait<sic> the furniture down." She ended her letter with "Words of love. Your girl."

The next year, Margaret found a position with a family in Evanston, Illinois. Edgar Chevy "E.C." Chase, his wife Cleda and their 7-year-old son Chevy lived on North Michigan Avenue, a short train-ride away from Margaret's high school. E.C. was a fuel engineer for the Chicago office of Consolidated Coal, the nation's largest producer of bituminous (black) coal. Margaret looked after Chevy and was paid $2.50 a week.

"Back then, we didn't call them 'au pair girls' like we do now," she recalled years later. "We were just sort of a hired hand, but they treated me as nice as if I'd been their own daughter." After Margaret graduated from high school, in the spring of 1936, Cleda asked her to stay on. They would help her get into college. But Margaret had to decline. "You've stayed in the North long enough," Haskins told her. "You need to come home."

By then, Margaret's parents were getting back on their feet. Haskins had gone back to farming and Mae had begun a new career, as Osceola correspondent for the *Blytheville Courier-News*. Her stories also appeared in the *Memphis Press-Scimitar* and *Commercial Appeal*, and the *Arkansas Gazette* in Little Rock. It wasn't a lot of money, of course, but she loved the work and later became a regular reporter and society editor of the hometown paper, *The Osceola Times*. In later years, Mae was the first woman member of the Arkansas State Southern Baptist Board, and served as president of the Osceola Progressive Club, part of a nationwide movement of women's clubs that endeavored to influence public policy on issues ranging from education to child labor.

Margaret wanted to become a dentist like her half-brother, Oleander Harrell "Hack" Jones, 10 years older, who had a practice in McAllen, Texas. She wanted to do her undergraduate work at Baylor, like he had. Her parents could not afford to send her to the exclusive Baptist college, 600 miles from home in Waco, Texas. Undeterred, Mae wrote to Baylor University President Pat Morris Neff, a former Texas governor, asking if her daughter could work her way through college. Neff responded and offered Margaret a job in the girl's infirmary to cover her tuition.

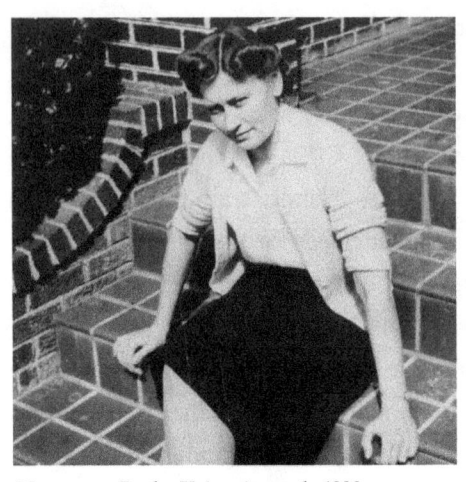

Margaret at Baylor University, early 1939

In the fall of 1938, at the beginning of her junior year at Baylor, Margaret enrolled in a two-year pre-dentistry course. But she soon realized that the $90 she earned each month at the infirmary was barely enough to cover her room and board and living expenses, much less her tuition and books. Hack suggested that she come to Houston and train as a medical technician at the old Jefferson Davis Hospital. Then the next fall, she could enroll in the Texas Dental College. As a medical technician, she would be qualified to teach in the college's bacteriology lab, and she could earn more than she was making in the Baylor infirmary. In those days, admission to the dental school did not require a baccalaureate degree.

So that's what she did. "Thank goodness for the Depression," Margaret would often say, "or I probably wouldn't have amounted to a hill of beans." Mae recalled a letter she received from Willie Dawson, wife of the prominent Southern Baptist preacher, the Rev. James M. Dawson. Mrs. Dawson was well known for her work on behalf of women's mission programs and higher education. When Margaret was a sophomore at Baylor, Mrs. Dawson had heard her speak to the Business Woman's Circle in Waco about a Christian's responsibility in race relations.

"Her message showed a deep concern for better conditions and opportunities for the Negroes," Mrs. Dawson wrote. "This sincere young girl was planning to give her life in Christ's service and proposed to use her hands in delicate ministry as a doctor of dentistry."

Mae stifled a sob as she looked at her daughter's broken body. Just two more years, and Margaret would have begun that lifetime of service. "Now what?" she whispered, her faithfulness faltering for a moment. "What's to become of my girl?"

The operation to amputate Margaret's arms was scheduled for 11 a.m. on Thursday, July 3. The operating team was made up of four surgeons, including Margaret's brother-in-law, Dr. William Burton "Bill" Thorning, who was married to her older sister, Louise.

Early that morning, however, an artery burst on her left side. The doctors couldn't stop the flow. Margaret was bleeding to death. Haskins, who was in the room at the time, collapsed. As Margaret was rushed to the operating room, one of the surgeons told Hack, "She's never coming off the table alive."

The surgeon wasn't being mean; he just didn't want to give the family false hope. But Margaret confounded his expectations. She survived the operation, although she continued to need a lot of blood. Six days later, on July 9, Mae wrote in one of her dispatches to *The Osceola Times* that "Miss Margaret slept well the night before, and was given her eighth blood transfusion during the day ... The chief danger is infection the next two or three days, and if she passes this crisis, she may live."

Shortly thereafter, Haskins returned home, while Mae continued to hold vigil by her daughter's side. She continued to file reports with the *Times* and the *Courier News*, which on July 22 reported that Margaret's condition was "definitely improved," although "she has not yet been told of the death of her fiancé."

The reference to fiancé seems a bit presumptuous, especially since the couple was not engaged. Yet among dozens of telegrams sent to Margaret and her parents by family and friends from around the country during those first horrible days after the accident, one was wired from Berkeley, California.

"Am sending flowers to Margaret. If you wish, you might let her think they came from Lou. Love and great sympathy, Jeanne." That was Lou's sister, Jeanne Crutchett.

Perhaps Mae telling the world her version of events was an attempt to bolster her spirits, by chronicling Margaret's fight to survive. With each story she wrote, Mae was walking into a new life—away from Osceola, and into a strange world of hospitals and big cities. In a sense, she was being transformed as radically as was her daughter.

Since Margaret's birth, Mae had tried to cultivate in her daughter the same faith and unshakeable sense of self she held for herself deep inside. Now she prayed that her daughter would survive, and if she did, that she would be able to accept what had happened to her.

She prayed that Margaret would have the strength to go on living.

Chapter Two
Learning to Swim Again

Margaret began to come back to herself around the third week in July. Although she was still in pain, she no longer screamed out for another shot of morphine. Drifting in and out of consciousness in her sunny hospital room, filled with bouquets of flowers, she was in a dreamlike state. Alone for a few moments, she imagined herself back at school, attending the clinic where she practiced filling cavities on a manikin, making dentures, and socializing with her friends.

And then there was the big Saturday night dance the previous November at the Glenbrook Country Club, where she had first dated Lou, a transfer student from the University of California, Berkeley. The next day she penned a letter to her parents telling them all about it. First, they'd gone to Ellen Wellensiek's house for cocktails and then to the club. "I had a grand rush," she wrote. "The dance ended at 1:30—then we went to the swank night club—the music stopped there at 2:30—then we had coffee and came home—but the coffee had awakened me up, so I even read the paper when I got home—and slept until 12 o'clock—such a heathen …"

Margaret smiled at the memory. Then, as she aroused from her reverie, her thoughts turned to her "casualty count."

"I'd lost time and money that I needed to get ready for my third year of dental school," she told the Rev. Dr. John Warren Steen Jr., a pastor and Christian journalist from Nashville, for an article for Billy Graham's *Decision* magazine years later. "Worst of all, I'd suffered excruciating pain in my arms. As I thought of the torment I'd been through, I glanced down. My chest was covered with a towel, as if a dentist had draped it just before extracting some teeth. At that moment, a gust of July wind blew through the open hospital window and uncovered me. I stared in horror."

When Mae returned to her daughter's room a few minutes later, she found Margaret gasping, sputtering, her face red and ragged with tears.

"How could this happen?" she screamed. "Why did you let them take my arms? You didn't even ask me!"

Mae started to explain, but Margaret cut her off.

"What about Lou?" she demanded.

Mae looked down and shook her head sadly.

"No!!!"

Years later, Margaret recalled being overcome with grief and weeping. "I knew Christ as my Savior. I had received Him into my life when I was 12," she said. "Now I prayed to die. Bereaved, fighting phantom pain that raced down to fingertips I didn't have, and depressed, I almost lost my faith. But God challenged me."

A couple of days later, her mother announced that she had a visitor. In walked Dean Elliott. His angular face, receding hairline, and pencil-thin mustache usually gave him an imposing presence. But on this day, he came to the side of Margaret's bed, smiling broadly.

"We're making plans for your return to school," he said.

"Are you crazy?" she scoffed.

"We've got lots of dentists with hands," the dean responded. "We could use one with a good head. You're coming back to school, and you are going to graduate with your class."

She could continue to teach the freshman lab class, he continued, and he would raise her salary to cover her tuition.

"Margaret," her mother added softly, "the time will come when you will see that there is still a purpose in your life. You will realize that you have a mission."

Margaret wasn't ready to hear that. She shook her head defiantly, as hot tears she could no longer wipe away burned down her cheeks.

"I can remember wasting a lot of time, thinking that if I prayed hard enough, I could wake up with my arms, that God would perform a miracle," she told author Dennis Wholey years later. "I don't doubt that He could have if it served a purpose, but it would be upsetting the laws of nature to do it. I can remember saying, 'I don't see why God let me live. I'll be a millstone around my family's neck and a burden on society ...'

"I don't think it was my faith in God that got me through," she continued. "I wasn't mature enough. It was my faith in my mother's faith in God. She had such a strong faith. When I would be dissolved in tears and grief, and when I'd quit crying and verbalized my fears, my mother would say, 'If God spared your life when 20 doctors said you couldn't live, there has to be a reason for it. You may be old and gray before you know it, and you may not know it until you get to Heaven, but it's your responsibility to keep looking, keep searching for it.'"

Margaret never gave up on God. But that doesn't mean she didn't challenge Him, either, by "putting out the fleece" in her prayers. The expression comes from the Book of Judges. Gideon puts God to the test before agreeing to lead a revolt against the Midianites. "I will place a wool fleece on the threshing floor," he tells God. If the next morning "there is dew only on the fleece and all the ground is dry, then I will know that You will save Israel by my hand, as You said." In Margaret's case, the fleece was the qualifying exams she'd taken in mid-June for her junior year. "Lord," she whispered in a hoarse, quavering voice. "I can't take these exams over. If you want me to stay in school, send me passing grades."

A few days later, the dean paid another visit. This time he had an envelope in his hand. He pulled out a sheet of paper and showed it to Margaret. She'd passed. Elliott placed the test results on the small table next to her bed. As he turned to go, he said softly, "Margaret, don't think that God is punishing you for something."

"That never occurred to me," she responded. "I think of God as a heavenly Father, a loving Father. Why would he punish me? I was at the wrong place at the wrong time. I don't think it was God's will that I'd go through life without my arms. It happened, pure accident."

At last, Margaret could see a ray of light piercing the gloom of her predicament. She knew that without hands, she could not become a practicing dentist. But she could teach. She was good at that. She would become a teacher of public health dentistry.

There is no simple recipe for recovery from the kind of trauma Margaret had experienced, no straight-line readjustment to a new life without arms. But her friends helped enormously. As soon as she was able, she welcomed in a flood of visitors, including her classmates. They helped her regain her characteristic sunniness and good humor.

When informed that among her blood donors were young men from France, Italy, and England, she quipped, "Well, I'll either come out fighting or be a League of Nations!"

Five weeks after the accident, Margaret was discharged from the hospital. She moved in with her sister Louise and her surgeon brother-in-law, Bill Thorning. Their three-bedroom home at 2906 Nottingham Street in Houston was about four miles from the dental school. Mae had returned to Osceola, but with the help of a maid, Louise fed her sister, helped her get dressed in the morning, and at the end of the day assisted with her bedtime routine. Once classes began in September, the family hired a dental assistant to help her with her course work.

Bill and Louise Thorning

At this point, Bill called a family conference. It was decided that no one would offer to help her in any way unless she asked for it first. "That was the hardest for my mother to stick to," Margaret recalled years later. "Her natural instinct was to do everything for me."

Margaret readily agreed to the family's decision. She was determined not to be a burden. She became a "master adapter" instead, forcing her feet and teeth and mouth to do almost everything her hands had once done—pull out a chair, open the car glove compartment, and even answer the telephone. She learned to write with a pen clenched between her teeth. When she read alone, she'd secure the page with a clothespin. As she neared the bottom of the page, she'd remove the clothespin with her teeth and turn the page with her tongue or nose.

Years later, she would put it this way: "Come hell or high water, you teach yourself to do things. You don't know how—you just do it."

One day, she announced she was going downtown to get a hair ribbon—alone. She wore a suit with large pockets to hold her purse and her purchases. Her mother put the bus fare in one pocket, so the driver could reach it easily. At the department store, the clerk put Margaret's purchases in one pocket and took her money from the other. But while that first excursion was an immense success, Margaret hated being stared at. So, she had most of her wardrobe made over into capes that completely covered her shoulders. Soon she was constantly running errands for the family and shopping for herself.

Margaret in her "disguise," late 1941

In early October 1941, a mere three and a half months after the accident, Margaret sent a long, typewritten letter to her parents that she had dictated to Louise, telling them about two new bonnets she'd purchased. "One is a pretty black one trimmed with red that fits very closely on my head so the wind will not take it off." Also, "I bought a pair of gold earrings, which make me look very Latin, but I fear Sister is going to wear them out before I get a chance to wear them!"

Margaret's subterfuge with the capes came to a screeching halt one evening, however, when, after boarding a bus, she asked the driver to reach into the pocket of her cape for the fare.

"What's the matter with your hands?" he growled. "Can't you do it yourself?"

Margaret froze, not knowing what to do or say. Her cheeks burned with embarrassment. For a moment she thought she would have to get off the bus and walk back home. But "giving up" was not part of Margaret's vocabulary. That day she wore a cape that tied at the throat, and which covered her sleeveless dress. Without a word she bent her head, scrunched her shoulders until she could grab the end of the tie with her teeth and pulled. The cape slid off her shoulders and billowed to the floor of the bus.

The driver's mouth dropped open and his eyes widened. Behind her passengers gasped with astonishment. "Oh my God!" one woman exclaimed. "She doesn't have any arms!"

For a few seconds, no one moved. Then from the back of the bus strode a young man in jeans and a baseball jersey. He picked up Margaret's cape, placed it over her shoulders and tied it securely under her chin. She looked at him, her eyes glistening. Seeming to understand, he reached into the left pocket of her cape, secured the fare, and handed it to the driver.

"Thank you," she mouthed inaudibly.

The young man tipped his cap. "Yes, ma'am," he said, and returned to his seat.

Amid the murmurs and some tittering of the passengers around her, Margaret found a seat by herself near the front of the bus so she could make a hasty exit. She completed her errand, but that was the last day she wore a cape. She knew she had to face up to the fact that people were always going to stare.

"There were times when I faltered," she admitted to Houston-based writer Louise Berthold, who wrote a feature about her in April 1943 for a women's magazine. But Margaret added that the kindness of her family and friends and the faith they had in her "bolstered up my courage and made me go on."

With the Japanese attack on Pearl Harbor in December 1941, the United States was pulled into the worldwide conflict that had already darkened much of Europe and Asia. Hack joined the Navy Reserve Dental Corps. Before reporting to the Training Station in San Diego, Lieutenant O. Harrell Jones asked Margaret if she'd like to go with him to the Rotary Club banquet. Excited and honored, she accepted immediately. But later she had second thoughts.

"I just remembered that I can't feed myself," Margaret told her mother over the phone. "I'm afraid I'll be self-conscious having someone feed me in public. I'll tell Brother I can't go."

At Mae's urging she went anyway, wearing her prettiest dress, dreading what she imagined might happen. But she ended up delighting the Rotary Club members and their guests with her sweetness and charm.

The same thing had happened when she returned to school. "I was the only girl in a class of 24, and every one of those boys was like a big brother to me," Margaret recalled. The Psi Omega dental fraternity adopted her as a little sister.

"When I lay in the hospital fighting for my life, they gave their blood for numerous transfusions, and they kept my room literally filled with flowers," she said. "When I returned to my classes, one of them brought me home from school—others read my lessons aloud or helped me with my themes. At lunch time they made me feel it was a privilege to feed me, and they even learned to repair my makeup and to pin up unruly locks of hair."

Margaret was beginning to understand that her disability was a gift in a way, for it invited those she met to be generous, to live outside of themselves, if only for a moment. She was beginning to understand that in her neediness and openness, she was giving her friends—and even strangers who responded to her with instinctive acts of kindness—something of much greater value than anything they could give or do for her.

Before the accident she was an excellent swimmer and, oh, how she loved to dance. When she told her mother how much she would miss those activities, Mae responded, "There's no reason why you shouldn't swim, Margaret, and dance too." Mae contacted the swimming instructor of the local YWCA, who worked out a lesson plan. Within a matter of weeks, using her legs to propel her, Margaret was able to swim the entire length of the pool and back.

Margaret also started going to dances again. "Far from being a wallflower," Berthold noted in her profile, "she is one of the most popular girls present. This is not because she incites pity, for so completely does she forget her handicap that she compels others to (ignore it, too). Indeed, since her dresses are made with long sleeves, seeing her for the first time on a dance floor, sparking with gaiety and wit, and surrounded by a group of young people, you would merely think, 'What an attractive girl!'"

By now, Margaret was used to strangers extending their hands in greeting when they met her, then hurriedly pulling their hands back when they realized she had nothing to shake with. To dispel the embarrassment, she'd respond with a joke, such as, "I'm sorry, but I left my arms at home today." And then she and her new friends would laugh heartily, together.

"Although we cannot know the mental battle which Margaret must have fought after her injury," her mother told a reporter, "she is now completely at ease concerning her disability."

When Berthold marveled at her cheerfulness, Margaret responded, "Just because I lost my arms, there's no reason why I should lose my sense of humor, too. Next to my faith in God, I consider that the most important asset in overcoming my handicap. Besides, since Mother and the rest of my family have been so wonderful through all this, I'd certainly be ungrateful if I didn't try to be as cheerful as possible. Not that my battle is entirely won. There are still periods of heartache, but they're growing farther and farther apart."

That doesn't mean she left the accident completely behind her. In November, three weeks before the attack on Pearl Harbor, Margaret filed a lawsuit against the Houston Lighting and Power Company, alleging negligence because the company had allowed its power line to sag dangerously low over the bay where the sailboat's mast made contact. In May, she was awarded $37,500, one of the largest judgments ever awarded by the Harris County District Court.

Although Lou's family did not join the lawsuit, his sister Jeanne continued to write, at one point sending Margaret some of the snapshots that had been taken of the two of them in happier times. For the rest of her life, Margaret would hold a special place in her heart for her first love.

Just as her brother-in-law had instructed during the family conference, Dean Elliott admonished her fellow students to let her fend for herself as much as she was able. Yet his office door was always open to her. To help her complete essay examinations, he'd send his secretary to sit with her in the hall outside the classroom and record Margaret's answers as she dictated them. "There were times when I felt so low, I could crawl under his door without mussing my hair," Margaret recalled years later. But "he had the capacity to inspire people."

"You're going to graduate," he'd tell her when she was feeling particularly low and blue. "You're going to get your master's degree and make a living teaching. And you're going to marry, too." After a few such encouraging words, Margaret said she would leave his office "feeling 10 feet tall!"

During her junior and senior years at the dental college, Margaret would stand beside her classmates as they performed extractions, fillings, and root canals, yearning to be able to do what they were doing. She felt her hands and fingers for a long time, even though they were gone.

One day she received a call from Dr. Albert P. Westfall, a part-time faculty member at the Texas Dental College, who would go on to establish the orthodontics program after the college became part of the University of Texas. He told her that he needed help with patient education, and he had a foot device installed in his office so she could answer the phone.

"He needed me like a hole in the head," Margaret told a reporter years later, "but he knew I needed something to fill up the empty hours."

What empty hours? In addition to her regular coursework and now part-time job, Margaret took classes in diction, radio speaking, and Spanish, figuring those skills and a second language would be useful for a public health career, especially if she stayed in Texas. She also returned to teaching freshman bacteriology, only this time with a young man at her side who wrote her lecture notes on the blackboard and took the roll.

And what about Ellen, whose quick action to break the high-voltage current with an oar probably saved Margaret's life on that horrible day? There are hints in Margaret's correspondence that they kept up their friendship for a while, and Ellen sent a wedding gift, a pretty blouse, when Margaret married in 1946. But eventually, like college friends often do, they parted ways. After graduation, Ellen went into private practice and did pioneering work in cosmetic dentistry and the use of plastics in restorative procedures.

Without arms but with a good head on her shoulders, Margaret would have to find a different path.

Chapter Three
Now It Is Up to You

In the summer of 1942, Margaret and her mother traveled to Minneapolis, Minnesota, so she could be fitted with artificial arms.

Minneapolis was the place to go for prosthetics. Five hundred miles from the source of the mighty Mississippi River, the city surrounds a natural waterfall named for Saint Anthony of Padua, the patron saint of lost things and lost people. And, one might add, lost limbs.

In the mid-19th century, Minneapolis was home to dozens of sawmills, paper mills, woolen mills, cotton mills and flour mills, all powered by St. Anthony Falls. Milling is a hazardous undertaking, however, and during the 1880s a new industry emerged—manufacturing artificial limbs for mill employees and others who had been maimed on the job, on the railroad or in battle. By 1938, even in the depths of the Great Depression, Minneapolis boasted nine artificial limb companies with combined sales that year of $200,000—an amount equivalent to nearly $3.7 million today.

In the early days, artificial limbs were nearly always made of wood. Because wood was rationed during World War II, manufacturers switched to other materials, mostly plastic and metal. Yet the artificial arms made for Margaret in Minneapolis were awkward, heavy, and uncomfortable, and she couldn't make them work. She rarely wore them. "I do like most people with false teeth," she'd joke. "I wear them in the drawer!"

By early 1943 Margaret had satisfied the requirements for graduation from dental school. Her mother and Dean Elliott encouraged her to participate in the commencement exercises that spring with the rest of her class. The dean had another motive. He knew Margaret would attract more attention to the Texas College of Dentistry, which was joining the University of Texas system that year. Not only was she the only female in her graduating class, as far as he knew, she was about to become the only armless dentist in the world.

Margaret (center) and the class of 1943. Dean Elliott, with mustache, is in the front row.

Already news of her remarkable achievement had spread far beyond Houston. She'd received more than 100 telegrams, long distance calls, letters, gifts, and flowers from friends, fraternities, and state dental societies from all over the United States and even Canada. She was deluged by offers to speak at luncheons hosted by business and service organizations. A women's magazine published in New York called *She* had commissioned Houston-based writer Louise Berthold to write a feature about Margaret for its April 1943 issue. The Associated Press assigned a reporter and photographer to the story, which would be distributed to 3,000 newspapers nationwide. And Universal Motion Pictures, which produced newsreels for movie theater audiences, was sending a film crew.

Margaret was reluctant at first. She did not want to become a freak or an object of pity. But Elliott encouraged her to consider it.

"Margaret," he said, "you must realize that your courageous determination in the face of your handicap is news. It will be news all your life, and every place you go you will be greeted by requests for interviews. You must decide now what your course will be."

Eventually Margaret agreed to be filmed, but only because she saw it as an opportunity to serve others—and to teach.

"So many of our young men have been turned down by the Army and Navy because of defective teeth," she told a reporter. "I am now more convinced than ever that I want to continue in this field. Particularly with children, I want to be instrumental in teaching them the importance of good teeth in connection with sound health."

Springtime in the South comes early, and Houston in mid-March was bursting, as Mae described it, with "blooming azaleas shoulder high, redbud and dogwood, green palms and green lawns." In her letter, which was read at the next meeting of the Osceola Progressive Club and later published in the local newspaper, Mae described how "every vacant lot in the city is being planted in Victory Gardens; often three or four neighbors are cultivating a nearby big lot, dividing it into equal sections; the men come home from the offices, get into slacks and work 'til dark, all conducive to good health and good old-fashioned neighborliness."

Victory gardens were encouraged by the government to increase the domestic supply and thus lower the price of vegetables needed to feed the troops. By May 1943, an estimated 18 million victory gardens were generating about a third of the national yield of tomatoes, carrots, potatoes, and onions, rivaling the production of commercial farms.

"Every vacant lot in Osceola (should) be planted," Mae urged in her letter. "All this comes under the department of War Service."

Hack could not attend Margaret's graduation. The previous June he'd been called to active duty, and his unit was attached to the Marine Air Corps. But he sent a letter from the Marine Aviation Base in San Diego.

Hack in uniform, 1941

"Hello Darling," he began, as he always did. "I am liking my duty more all the time … Don't think I did so bad yesterday for my first day of work, put in 16 fillings and did a surgical extraction. It is all rather primitive but interesting … You should see me in my Marine outfit, I can't get used to it. Everyone says it looks swell, but then of course most everyone is polite … Seems that I must go to work. Be a sweet girl and remember that I love you. Hack."

The commencement celebration began on Friday afternoon, March 19, with a formal tea hosted by Margaret's sister, Louise, at her home in honor of her mother and sister and the rest of the graduates and members of the college faculty. The baccalaureate service was held on Sunday morning at St. Paul's Methodist Church, and on Monday afternoon the dean and Mrs. Elliott hosted a reception at the Dental College Library.

Graduation exercises began at 8 p.m. Monday night at the South Main Baptist Church with a processional march of the Marine Hymn, "Stars and Stripes Forever" and "Anchors Aweigh." Dr. Chauncey Leake, dean of the University of Texas Medical Branch, delivered the commencement address on "The Coordination of Medicine and Dentistry for War." Then Elliott came to the podium to present the candidates for the degree of Doctor of Dental Surgery.

As flashbulbs popped and cameras whirred, 25-year-old Margaret Jones walked onto the pulpit in her graduation cap and long-sleeved gown to a burst of enthusiastic applause. Elliott raised her diploma, which was tied to a white silk cord, and draped it around her neck. Afterwards, Margaret's parents, sister and other family members grouped around her as the cameras rolled.

The newsreel showed Margaret standing beside a dental chair in the clinic, directing students in the bacteriology clinic, and walking with others on campus. It was released to movie theaters in June as part of a series entitled "Person Oddities in the News." At the Gem Theatre in Osceola that June, it preceded the just-released feature film "Crash Dive," starring Tyrone Power and Ann Baxter. The newsreel also was distributed as a morale booster to military hospitals and to troops fighting in the Pacific.

Among those who watched the short film that showed Margaret in the laboratory and receiving her diploma was the proud family with whom she had lived while she finished high school in Chicago. Chevy, who referred to himself as Margaret's "little brother," thanked her for sending a book of piano themes for his 16th birthday. He had recently taken up piano again.

His mother Cleda wrote, "The movie of you was so good to see, however it was almost too much for me ... There isn't a day goes by I don't think of you and say a little prayer for so wonderful a girl as you certainly are. I am so glad you have decided what you intend to do in the future ... My Dear, take good care, and say a little prayer for me once in a while."

Even before her story was splashed across the big screen, Margaret was awash in "fan mail" from soldiers at the front and in field hospitals around the globe. Her mother filled a scrapbook with their letters. Determined to answer as many as she could, Margaret purchased a Dictaphone to record her voice on a wax cylinder, and in that way dictated letters to be typed later by Mae.

One handwritten letter dated the day of her graduation was sent from a military hospital in Fort Lauderdale, Florida.

"I am a radioman in the Navy," George F. Chamberlain began. "About two months ago, my ship got into a scrap with three submarines not far from the Panama Canal. We got two of them but the third got us. In the process, I was injured by a falling mast and shortly afterward lost both legs. I was very discouraged for a long while, although soon I will walk again on artificial limbs. I figured that a man with no legs was absolutely helpless. Then a couple of days ago, I read a small article in the *Miami Herald* telling how you, with no arms, had earned a degree in dental surgery. Since then, I have been very much inspired by your story. If you overcame your obstacle, then I am sure I can mine ...

"I am (or was) 6 feet tall, brown hair, blue eyes, weight 181," he continued. "... I am crazy about music, all kinds, and was formerly a radio announcer and musician. Played trumpet and trombone with the Glen Gray and the Casa Loma Orchestra for a year. Am 25 years old and single.

"Now it is up to you."

Margaret must have burst out laughing at George's bold proposal. He hadn't even met her, didn't even know what she looked like except for a grainy black-and-white photo in the newspaper! But she responded, as she always did, only with kind, encouraging words. In a letter she dictated to her mother, she told him how fortunate he was that some of the things he did before the war, including being a radio announcer and a member of a popular swing band, did not require feet.

Within two weeks, another handwritten letter arrived.

"I can see why you stuck it out, instead of giving up and retiring to some dark corner to reap self-pity for the rest of your life," George began. "You undoubtedly have spirit which, coupled with faith, means everything. The truth of the matter is that before my enlistment in the good old USN and subsequent accident, I was a loud, boisterous individual, moderately successful but without any responsibility. Since then, I have settled down a bit (naturally) and begun to plan. I know that if I had used intelligence before, I could have been near the 'top' in radio. My musical talents are not quite that good, but at 17 years of age, I was a staff announcer for CBS. You may have heard me on the 'Camel Caravan' (*a musical variety radio program sponsored by Camel cigarettes*) ... At 22 I was working for a small 250-watt station in Florida for just 20% of what I made at 17. This was due almost entirely to my attitude and lack of responsibility. Now that I have had the time to think it over, I may be able to climb back again. And after seeing (or rather, reading) of your accomplishments, I do not feel handicapped.

"Margaret, you're OK."

Then, his mood lightening with every scrawl on the page, he continued. "I was thinking of having my 'peg legs' equipped with built-in pogo-sticks so as to get around in a hurry. That would give me quite an advantage. Don't you think so? Or maybe I should use roller skates run by a concealed electric motor in each ankle. Suggestions would be appreciated ... Whenever you can talk your mother into writing another volume my way, I can assure you I will be most happy to receive it. Meanwhile, best of luck.

"Your friend, George."

What George did with the rest of his life shall remain a mystery. But clearly, on this day at least, he had chosen not to withdraw into a dark corner of self-pity. Nor was he the only wounded soldier who was touched by Margaret's bravery, good humor, and hope.

"Thus, she continues to be a real missionary," Mae wrote.

Louise Berthold, the writer, agreed. "Deeply religious, Margaret possesses a serenity and a beauty of soul seldom seen in one so young," she noted in her article. "You cannot look into her clear blue eyes without absorbing a little of the quiet courage shining there—(and) without feeling ashamed for having grumbled at some small disappointment."

Chapter Four
Freedom From Fear

Margaret did not let her recent brush with fame derail her career plans. Immediately after graduation, she spent four days taking the Texas State Board Examination in Dentistry. She was determined to earn a master's degree in public health and become a teacher of dentistry. But to do that, she would have to go back to Baylor University and finish her Bachelor of Arts degree.

She took a European history course over the summer of 1943 while staying with Louise and Bill in New Orleans. He was stationed at a hospital there during the war. "We bought a Dictaphone," Margaret recalled years later. "I would read and outline a chapter and dictate it with the Dictaphone, and Sister would type it at night, and we would mail it to the professor."

In September, she and her mother found an apartment on South 8th Street in Waco so that she could attend school full-time. Margaret took her exam in European History orally, but for the other courses, Mae served as her daughter's secretary, taking dictation as she read her assignments or answered questions in written examinations, and typing out her themes and papers. Among her course work was a class in Interpretative Reading for Radio, taught by Sara Lowrey, chair of the Speech Department.

Lowrey would become an important influence and a life-long friend.

Gracious yet forceful, with flowing hair she'd allowed to turn naturally gray and piercing dark eyes, Sara Lowrey had chaired the department since 1923, the same year she earned her master's degree in public discourse from the university. As chair, she instituted programs in oral interpretation, radio, and speech correction.

"To many generations of Baylor students, Sara Lowrey was the epitome of the lady, the scholar, the teacher," Gretchen P. Thomas, her secretary, wrote years later in a profile published in a Baylor University magazine. She required of her students three essentials of good speech—flawless articulation, a pleasant voice, and a fastidiously erect posture. The article quoted fellow teacher Dorothy Hanson, who said, "The most remarkable thing about her teaching is her ability to reach into an individual and pull out the strength and skill no one knew was there." Margaret, who also was quoted in the article, said Lowrey "made me believe in the impossible."

At the beginning of the fall term Lowrey profiled Margaret for the student newspaper, *The Baylor Lariat*. The aim of the front-page article published on October 1 was to ease Margaret's return to college life, and as Lowrey often put it to her students, "prepare you for the future."

The encouragement worked. Margaret immersed herself enthusiastically in college life. She was elected president of the International Relations Club, one of Baylor's largest organizations, became active in Psi Chi, the honor society for psychology students, and spoke to many campus and city groups.

Later that month, Margaret was one of four students chosen to speak in Waco Hall on the "Four Freedoms" during the Baylor Religious Hour, which offered "an hour of quiet devotion and inspiration" on Wednesday nights. The Four Freedoms, as enunciated by President Roosevelt during his 1941 State of the Union address, were Freedom of Speech, Freedom of Worship, Freedom from Want and Freedom from Fear. Margaret's topic was the fourth freedom for, as she explained to a reporter, "I have a speaking acquaintance with Fear."

The transcript of Margaret's talk was reprinted in the *Lariat*'s October 29 edition. "Since the beginning of time, man has had to battle fear, making the world safer and safer," she began. "Now nations have brought armed fear into the world to destroy this safety. The world is not free from fear, but it can be free. As Americans, we must not betray the trust of other nations by putting our selfishness first. Freedom from fear is not freedom from responsibility."

Margaret entered her talk in Baylor's Inter-American Affairs Discussion Contest, which highlighted the importance of Pan-American relations. The contest was sponsored by the U.S. Office of the Coordinator of Inter-American Affairs, established in 1941 by executive order of the president to counter Fascist and Nazi propaganda in Latin America. Margaret and James Leo Garrett Jr., a Baylor junior, won the contest that year. They received certificates signed by the agency's coordinator, Nelson Rockefeller, grandson of billionaire John D. Rockefeller, who went on to serve as governor of New York and Gerald Ford's vice president.

"I was very well pleased and happy to learn that you did so well in the Inter-American contest," Dean Elliott wrote from Houston in February 1944 after the awards were announced. "It shows that I was not so far wrong when I said you had it in you—if you wanted to do it."

Two-and-a-half years earlier, Elliott had shined a light of hope on a young woman who had nearly lost her will to live. Now, in this and in a series of letters that followed, he continued to offer sage advice and fatherly support to Margaret, who was weighing her options for the future. She was thinking about getting a master's degree in public health, or—flush with her recent success as a political speaker—running for a seat in the Texas House of Representatives.

"I don't know about the position in the State Legislature," he cautioned. But either way, "I am sure that it will not be long until you find that there is no such thing as stage fright," he wrote. "After all, who cares whether the stage becomes frightened or not? So far as you are concerned, the word 'fright' should not be in your vocabulary."

In July 1944, Margaret appeared on the college radio station, KWBU, on a program hosted by Lowrey about people with disabilities. "Every handicapped person desires to be treated as a normal individual," Margaret began. "In many instances a person can return to his same field of work or a related field as I have been able to do. But in a great number of cases, our young soldiers who are returning to us minus an arm or a leg and who may not have been trained in any particular field must be given special training for some position and an opportunity to return to normal social and business life.

"The public can do a great deal to help our wounded men make a comeback. In fact, it's up to the public," she said. "The men make the necessary adjustment in the hospital, but they dread their first contacts with family, friends, and the public in general. The public should, first of all, accept them and treat them as other normal people ... The public must not be too solicitous but must leave them alone to do what they can on their own ... Write letters to the wounded, assuring them of a welcome home ... but don't be too soft on them."

In addition to her speeches and papers, Margaret also became known as the "Sweetheart of Maimed Veterans" for her regular visits to veterans who were being treated for their wounds in the Army's McCloskey General Hospital in nearby Temple, a few miles south of Waco. Activated in June 1942, the hospital was named for the late Major James A. McCloskey, the first regular Army doctor to lose his life in the war. The hospital was one of the Army's largest general hospitals and specialized in orthopedic cases, amputations, and neurosurgery. At its peak, more than 5,000 wounded soldiers were being treated in its wards.

Nearly every weekend, Margaret would stroll up and down the long corridors, chatting with patients in their beds, on crutches, and in wheelchairs. As she passed along, men who'd lost their arms, legs, hands, or feet proudly showed off their "pros"—the prosthetics made for them in the hospital's brace shop. Years later, Lowrey recalled accompanying Margaret on one of her hospital visits. "As Margaret passed down the aisle between the beds, she spoke with ease to the servicemen, sometimes sitting on the edge of the bed ... It seemed to me that I could see courage coming into the faces of the men."

By the summer of 1944, Margaret, who had just turned 27, had completed all the requirements for the bachelor's degree, majoring in Zoology with a minor in Psychology. On August 16th, she joined 63 other graduates in the commencement exercises at Baylor University. Presenting the diplomas was Baylor President Pat Morris Neff, the former Texas governor who also was current president of the Southern Baptist Convention. At 72, Neff was still a handsome man. His firm jaw and steely eyes seemed undimmed by time.

As Margaret walked across the stage in Waco Hall to receive her diploma,

Neff addressed the audience. "No one has lived the abundant live more fully," he said, his right arm outstretched in her direction. "No one has stimulated faint hearts more. No one on the Baylor campus has radiated happiness and inspiration more than this young woman who exemplifies culture, courage, and character."

By then, Margaret was standing quietly beside him, her cheeks flaming. Neff turned to face her. "In appreciation of her as one of Baylor's daughters," he concluded. "I confer this degree upon her, placing it about her neck."

Margaret's parents, who were seated near the front of the assembly, no doubt had tears in their eyes as President Neff recognized their daughter's resilience and sacrifice in such a stirring way. He honored them as well. During much of the past three years, Mae had been away from her husband for extended periods, caring for her daughter and assisting her with her studies. Mae was able to do that only because of the patience and generosity of the man who had been with her and supported her through thick and thin for the past 31 years.

President Neff presents Margaret's diploma, 1944

If there were one word to describe Robert Haskin Jones, it was sturdy. Stocky in frame, his hands rough and calloused from years of farm work, he looked every bit the picture of the traditional man, a man of his time. But this gruff-voiced farmer had a tender heart. And he was intensely loyal. He was as straight and sturdy as an iron pole, unwavering and resolute in his love and dedication to his faith and his family.

He did manly things. When he wasn't working on the farm, he was fishing. He enjoyed a good cigar. But he also allowed Mae the freedom to do the things she wanted to do, to become the person she wanted to be, even if it meant they would be apart from each other for long periods of time. In that respect, one might say, Haskins was a man ahead of his time, an emancipated man. But that was only because he knew who he was and what he was put on this earth to do.

Haskins' steely self-confidence was a family trait, for he was descended from pioneers and trail blazers, men and women who broke new ground with their bare hands, and relying on no one else for assistance, brought forth bounty, the fruit of the earth, to nourish their families.

His grandparents and other members of the extended Jones family had emigrated from Virginia's Shenandoah Valley in the 1850s, settling in rural Brunswick in Shelby County, Tennessee, about 20 miles northeast of Memphis. His father, John M. Jones, was the third youngest of eight children. Born in 1879, Haskins was 7 when his grandfather, Stephen Jones Jr., passed away. No doubt as a young boy he heard hair-raising tales from his uncles, Russell, "Doc" and "Nat," about their service in the Confederate Army during the Civil War.

Robert Haskin Jones

The Joneses were thick in Brunswick; dozens are buried in the Pleasant Hill Cemetery. But Haskins made his own way in life. He left school after the fifth grade to work full-time as a logger and later as a farmer. By the age of 16, he'd moved on to Mississippi County, Arkansas, to clear great stands of timber from the 320 acres of land an uncle had bought for $1.03 an acre. Later he served as wood crew boss for the wealthy lumber company owner Robert E. Lee Wilson, helping him transform the forested swamps of the Mississippi Delta into some of the richest farmland in the country, much of it cultivated in cotton.

In its early days, the county seat, Osceola, was known as "Plumb Point," a designation given to it by steamboat captains who navigated the Mississippi, picking up timber and, of course, the voluminous bales of cotton that were the South's economic bedrock. In 1853, the town was renamed Osceola in honor of the famed Seminole chieftain, who 20 years earlier had fought the U.S. Army to prevent the removal of his people from their ancestral land in Florida during the Seminole Indian War.

According to the local newspaper, *The Osceola Times*, "Mr. Jones was one of the pioneers of this area, helping in the great job of clearing the timberland and draining the swamps to create this agricultural empire." Within a few years, the affable young man with the easy laugh had established himself as a farm manager on one of the county's biggest plantations and become, as the *Times* put it, "a popular personality."

Like Haskins, the former Georgia Mae Canady also hailed from southwest Tennessee, and she also was on her own at an early age. Born in 1892 into a family of ministers, teachers, and newspaper reporters, Mae started working as a schoolteacher at 16 to help support the family after her mother died of cancer. She taught farmers' sons and daughters how to read in a one-room schoolhouse in Dyersburg, and later across the Mississippi River in Blytheville, Arkansas.

In 1909, she took a teaching position in Osceola, clerking part-time at a grocery store. That's where she met Haskins, a widower who had a 3-year-old son named "Hack," short for Oleander Harrell.

Haskins' home and livelihood were in Carson Lake. The village had a schoolhouse, but no schoolteacher. It wouldn't be long before the boy would need one. Over the course of many months, Haskins cajoled Mae to relocate to Carson Lake. Finally, she relented, and in the fall of 1912, she became Harrell's first-grade teacher.

By then, Haskins, 33, and Mae, 20, had taken a fancy to each other. The courting continued until the spring of 1913, when a levee broke, flooding the town and ending the school year early. That gave the couple the opportunity to elope. They married on April 6 and spent their honeymoon at the iconic Peabody Hotel in Memphis.

Eight months later, on December 3, Louise was born in Osceola. Years later, the town's newspaper, *The Osceola Times,* would describe the union of Haskins and Mae Jones as "a good life, remembered with pleasure and romance."

Tragedy struck Haskins and Mae in July 1916 when their second child, a boy, died shortly after birth. "I never saw a sweeter baby in my life," a cousin wrote in a handwritten letter of sympathy. "After a while, you will see through it. God makes no mistakes. Heaven will seem nearer to you now that your precious Babe is there."

The loss of a child made Margaret's healthy arrival a year later more dear—especially for her father.

Haskins would always keep a special place in his heart for Margaret. He could still see her on a Sunday afternoon, scampering through the woods to gather walnuts, hickory nuts, and wild pecans. On winter mornings, she'd wave to him as Louise drove their horse and buggy to school. Mae would put hot bricks in the buggy to keep the girls' feet warm during their six-mile trek along bumpy dirt roads to Carson Lake.

Through the dark days of the Depression, when he'd lost his job and the family had to move in with relatives for a time, Margaret remained a beacon of pride and joy, even during the two years when she lived in Chicago while finishing high school.

And then came that dark day in June 1941 when she was nearly killed in a boating accident. Now she was leaving him once more. Margaret's application to the master's degree program in public health at the University of Michigan had been accepted. She and Mae would move to Ann Arbor in the fall.

Haskins just had to smile and shake his head when he thought about it.

Michigan. Might as well be Siberia!

Who knew what trails his brave wife and daughter would blaze in a place so far away from home, or when they would return?

Only God knew.

Chapter Five
Red Pencil

Margaret initially wanted to go to Johns Hopkins University in Baltimore, Maryland, for her master's degree in public health. But then she heard about the University of Michigan and Dr. Kenneth A. Easlick, DDS, one of the nation's earliest and most influential dental educators. At the University of Michigan, he developed one of the first teaching programs in pedodontics, children's dentistry, as well as the nation's first graduate program in dental public health. He was a giant in the fields that Margaret felt called to enter—children's dental health and public health dentistry—and she yearned to learn under him if she could. So, she applied, and she was accepted.

It is quite possible, however, that Easlick chose Margaret as much as she chose Michigan. For like Margaret, he had more than a speaking acquaintance with fear.

Upon graduating from the University of Michigan in 1917, he was one of more than four million "Doughboys" who answered President Woodrow Wilson's call to "make the world safe for democracy" during World War I. His detached unit in the U.S. Army Ambulance Service was assigned to French forces and sent to the Western Front, where the gangly and naïve 25-year-old ambulance attendant witnessed some of the worst of man's inhumanity to man. He pulled soldiers from the battlefield whose limbs had been blown off by mortar shells, whose faces had been blistered and grotesquely disfigured by mustard gas and whose lungs had been seared by phosgene—chemical weapons employed by the Germans.

For valor in evacuating wounded French soldiers under heavy shellfire during a battle in September 1918, shortly before the November 11 Armistice, he was awarded the Croix de Guerre (War Cross). Once he returned home, he took a job with the Reynolds Spring Company in Jackson, Michigan, which made springs and seats for automobiles. But he was haunted by what he'd experienced during the war. So, in 1924, he returned to the University of Michigan and enrolled in the School of Dentistry. After earning his degree, he joined the dental school faculty and began a career he hoped would help make the world a better place.

Yet now it was happening all over again—a SECOND World War. This time Easlick's son David was in the thick of battle. As an infantry officer in the Army, David took part in D-Day, the storming of the beaches of Normandy on June 6, 1944, by an assault force of 24,000 American, British, and Canadian troops. The beaches were defended by heavy machine gun fire, landmines, and barbed wire barricades. By the end of that first day, more than 10,000 Allied troops had been killed or wounded. But they'd gained a foothold, and gradually were forcing the German army to retreat. God only knew where David was now. With every phone call, with every knock on the door, Dr. Easlick and his wife prayed they would not be given news that their son had been horribly wounded—or killed.

And then came Margaret's application.

Had it not been for Easlick, her application would have been rejected outright by the admissions committee. Dr. Henry Frieze Vaughan, the founding dean of the School of Public Health, didn't think she'd be able to do the work. "Well, I think we should give her a chance," Easlick told the committee. He'd seen this remarkable young woman with no arms at a workshop during an American Dental Association meeting in Houston. He'd read about her. She was an inspiration to everyone she met. She would be perfect for what Easlick had in mind—a transformation of public health through dentistry.

Some may call it coincidence that Easlick happened to see her at that workshop in Houston. "But here again, I feel like God had to have been in it," Margaret told a gathering of Baylor alumnae in San Antonio years later. "I think it's God, working to direct our lives."

In late October 1944, Margaret and her mother rented rooms in a house on Geddes Avenue in a leafy neighborhood adjoining the University of Michigan's Nichols Arboretum, a few blocks from the School of Public Health. The fall term began on November 2.

Easlick demanded excellence from his graduate students. He was best known for wielding his ever-present red pencil. "It was a rare person who could get a page past him without a red mark on it," one of his former graduate students, Dr. David F. Striffler, recalled in 1980. "He had an eagle eye for grammatical errors and misspellings." It was not just for the sake of accuracy, however. Easlick wanted his students to be able to present themselves to the public, in both their written and oral communications, "in as ideal a fashion as possible."

But he was anything but severe. A kind-faced man, Easlick was more nurturer than taskmaster. "He had a manner," Striffler wrote, "of looking up when you appeared at his open door, inviting you in, carefully seeing that you were seated comfortably, pushing aside the materials with which he was always busily engaged, putting down his pen or pencil (red, of course) and cocking his head like the RCA Victor terrier, and saying in effect, 'Now I am ready to listen to you – you have my full attention.' It never seemed as if you were bothering him ... He was always available to you."

Margaret was a diligent student. With Easlick's encouragement, and the help of her mother and fellow students, one of whom carbon-copied all his notes for her, she completed her course work in epidemiology, child and public health dentistry, economics, statistics, nutrition, and community health organization. "It was just amazing how kind people were," she recalled years later. "In one class the chairman of my thesis committee made notes for me to take home, and Mother would type them."

As 1945 dawned, and the wars in Europe and the Pacific grinded on, Margaret lacked only the completion of her thesis to get her master's degree in public health. But she still managed to have time for a social life.

"I was dating a man from Egypt who lived in the same house I did," she recalled. "He was a very handsome man from Cairo. I was infatuated with him."

Margaret realized their romance would be short-lived; Salah Taha was nearing the completion of his doctorate in bacteriology and planned an academic career back home. What she didn't know was that there was another young man waiting in the wings, one who was equally infatuated with her, and one who was fiercely determined to win her heart.

Martin "Marty" Chanin was a brilliant, 23-year-old graduate student in pharmaceutical chemistry from Newark, New Jersey. Born January 24, 1922, the son of a Jewish wholesale produce dealer, he'd skipped two grades in high school and graduated third in his class at age 16. After graduation, he lived with relatives in Philadelphia while he attended the University of Pennsylvania. Marty wanted to become a doctor but after graduation in 1942 could not get into medical school. In those days, most U.S. medical schools had a strict quota on the number of Jews they admitted, reflecting antisemitic and anti-immigrant attitudes that were prevalent after World War I. He decided to pursue organic chemistry as a career instead. He worked for a large pharmaceutical company, which sent him to the University of Michigan for his graduate studies.

Salah introduced him to Margaret in January 1945 during an open house at the student union. By then, Marty had already earned his master's degree and was within a year of completing his Ph.D. Too young for the draft when the United States entered the war in December 1941, Marty later received a deferment on account of his studies in science. In addition to his course work, he was a research assistant to Dr. Reuben L. Kahn, chief of the Clinical Laboratories at the University of Michigan Hospital, who was known internationally for developing the Kahn precipitation test for syphilis.

Marty's broad forehead, dark, bushy eyebrows that rode atop his spectacles and usually solemn mouth gave him a stern expression. But he also was quite the romantic. Years later, he would admit that he had fallen for this lovely, armless young woman even before he met her—after seeing her picture in the newspaper when she graduated from dental school. He became even more smitten when he saw her on campus. Margaret was on her way to the movies in January with her

Egyptian boyfriend and one of her women friends from school when they bumped into Marty for the first time. The introduction was awkward. "He looked like he was just off the boat," Margaret recalled. "He had on jeans and a stocking cap and all." That was that, until Salah finished his doctorate.

"As soon as he was out of town, Marty called me for a date," she said. "I thought, 'I don't want to go out.' He was as homely as hell. And he was shorter than I was." At first, she turned down his invitation to go to the movies. But when she considered how dull her evening would be, reading by herself, she changed her mind. After that first date, "he just absolutely made himself indispensable. If it was raining, he'd be there with an umbrella. He started including me in invitations to parties. He was underfoot every time I turned around."

About this time, Easlick recommended Margaret for a dental health educator position with the Charles Stewart Mott Foundation of Flint, Michigan.

Mott was a former Flint mayor and long-time director and vice president of the General Motors Company, which had been headquartered in Flint until its move to Detroit in the mid-1920s. According to its vision statement, the Mott Foundation was established in 1926 to affirm a world in which "every person was in partnership with the rest of the human race, and where each individual's quality of life is connected to the well-being of the community." To that end, Mott and Flint educator Frank J. Manley promoted a "community school" approach to meet diverse community needs, ranging from adult education and vocational training to health screenings, organized recreation, and civic events. That's why the foundation needed a dental health consultant.

During the 1940s, Flint's population swelled dramatically, driven by the influx of newcomers—many of whom were Black—seeking good-paying jobs on the automobile assembly line and in the defense industries. But greater economic opportunity did not translate into the freedom to choose where to live or where to send one's children to school. Indeed, Flint during those years became repressively segregated. Restrictive real estate covenants, federal mortgage redlining and other housing and development policies prevented most Blacks from buying or even renting homes outside of predominantly Black districts. To ensure that the city's public schools also remained separate, officials gerrymandered attendance districts, manipulated student transfer rules, and even built temporary schoolhouses to keep white and Black students from mingling.

For about a year, Margaret and her mother rented a house in Flint so she could make her rounds of the city's public, parochial, and Lutheran schools. "I did all sorts of things, preparing a manual for teachers," she recalled. "I went into the classroom to talk about health and prevention, that sort of thing, and also did a lot of talks to parent groups." It is likely that Margaret visited schools in both communities—white and Black. She likely was not aware of the role that racist housing and education policies played in the continued separation of Flint's communities. But she knew segregation when she saw it, for she had grown up with Jim Crow. And yet she most certainly approached the subject with her usual cheerful optimism. For her faith in a loving God, which she'd embraced since childhood and which sustained her still, was colorblind. If anything, she may have spent more time in communities where there was a greater need.

By May 1945, the war in Europe was over. FDR did not live to see the defeat of Hitler's Germany. He died on April 12 of a massive cerebral hemorrhage. His vice president, Harry Truman, now occupied the Oval Office. Japan's surrender was imminent: in early August, Hiroshima and Nagasaki were pulverized by the first military use of the atomic bomb.

Around this time, Margaret received a somber note from the family she lived with while she finished high school in Chicago. Her "little brother" Chevy, a freshman at Northwestern University, had died on August 3 following an emergency operation for acute appendicitis at the hospital in Evanston—three months shy of his 18th birthday. Chevy's death "nearly killed me," Margaret recalled years later. "At the time I was so bitter. I said, 'I'm never going to get attached to anybody's child.' He wrote me all the time when I was at Baylor. He would tell people he had a big sister down south in college."

Chevy Chase

There is no record of it, but Margaret certainly would have attended Chevy's funeral in Evanston. She came back with Chevy's prized possession, a 21-inch-long wooden "pond yacht" that he used to sail in the lagoon at Dawes Park. Edgar and Cleda Chase wanted her to have it.

Margaret was still mourning Chevy's death when another matter clamored for her attention—Marty finally had conjured up the courage to ask her to marry him. The answer, at least at first, was a strenuous "no."

Margaret felt marriage was impossible. Marriage meant children and the ability to care for them and make a home. "I was helpless," she told a reporter years later. "I couldn't visualize any man in his right mind marrying me."

Margaret also was determined to make her way in the world, on her own terms. But Marty persisted in his entreaties, for more than a year, even as she persisted in her refusals. "She said 'no' so many times I lost count," he quipped.

On one occasion, they were arguing on the steps of one of the schools in Flint. "I painted the blackest picture you can imagine—everything that could go wrong," she recalled years later. "Marty, if we married, we would probably have a child and you just can't count on always having help. There will be dishes in the sink and diapers to change. If help doesn't show up, what would I do?"

"Are you through?" Marty asked finally. "Now tell me, just where would I be while all this is happening?'"

That called her up short. Margaret had been prepared to continue with her refusals. But she was 27. More importantly, her mother was 53. Mae had been away from her husband and Osceola for much of the past three years. Who would take care of her if Mother could not? Margaret was acutely aware of the fragility of life. This only made her discussions with Marty even more difficult.

Yet just how could Marty believe that marrying an armless woman was going to work? It was not only her physical handicap; they were from opposite poles of the universe. He was four and a half years younger and a city boy from New Jersey. His mother and father were first-generation Jewish Americans—their parents had immigrated to escape the pogroms, the state-sanctioned destruction of Jewish villages, in late 19th century Russia and Ukraine. She was a Southern Baptist with deep roots in this country, the daughter of a cotton farmer from rural Arkansas. Marty was not particularly religious. Margaret was. He was a garrulous chemist who enjoyed the clash of wits with fellow students and his instructors. He was a tinkerer, too, an inventor of weird mechanical contraptions. She was a dentist with a budding career in public health. She thrived on meeting and conversing with people one on one.

They did have a few things in common: ambition, a strong dose of independence and a willingness to swim upstream against the social norms of the day. Marty loved her vivaciousness and, frankly, yearned to take care of someone with special needs. Margaret, in turn, appreciated his attentiveness, his little acts of kindness. When they were out together at a restaurant, he became the arms she didn't have, removing her coat, making sure she was seated comfortably, bringing food to her lips—as if that were the most natural thing to do on earth, and anticipating her need for a sip of water even before she knew she was thirsty. He treated her like she was the only other person in the room, like a queen. He was truly devoted to her.

And so, Margaret began to engage him. Her "noes" became "maybes." But first, there were some serious issues to work out before "maybe" became "yes." She did not want to give up her career. She wanted to be as independent as possible, to do things for herself. Yes, yes, Marty agreed. Eventually, she wanted to have children. How?

"I'll help you," he jumped in eagerly. "You'll see."

But the children must be brought up in the Christian church.

"Of course," he said.

1946 had scarcely begun when Margaret decided to change her answer to "yes." It was, Marty observed wryly to himself, his V-M Day. Victory in Europe had come and gone. So had the Victory over Japan. This was his Victory over Margaret's stubborn refusals. At last, he had won the heart of the beautiful girl in the photograph.

Six months after she accepted his proposal, and just 18 months after they met, Margaret and Marty recited their vows to each other. The wedding ceremony was held at the First Baptist Church in Ann Arbor at 8 p.m. on June 25, a Tuesday, the day after Marty earned his PhD in pharmaceutical chemistry. He organized it that way. He had earned both his master's degree and doctorate in just three years, for Marty was a very organized man.

Marty's parents, Philip and Minnie Chanin, did not attend the wedding. They were strongly opposed to the marriage. In fact, several months before the wedding Minnie had flown to Ann Arbor to talk Margaret out of marrying her son. She accused Margaret of trying to ruin his life; he would be saddled with having to take care of an armless wife.

Margaret didn't know what to say. It was Marty, after all, who had pleaded with her to marry him. Marty responded without hesitation.

"You're out of line, Mother," he said firmly. "It's time for you to go home."

For her part, Margaret was a gorgeous bride. Statuesque and quietly dignified, she walked down the aisle in a floor-length satin gown and veil that draped her shoulders nearly to the waist, adorned by a pearl necklace with matching earrings. In a professional photo, she is seated with a bouquet of roses and baby's breath in her lap. Her lips allow only the tiniest hint of a smile as she gazes steadily and confidently at the camera.

Margaret was met at the altar by her husband-to-be, who was wearing a white dinner jacket and black bowtie. Before them stood Dr. Franklin Hamlin Littell, director of the University's Lane Hall, to conduct the ceremony. No doubt Margaret wanted to be married in a Baptist church, but perhaps the pastor did not perform interfaith marriages. So, the couple asked Littell, a Methodist minister who they likely had met at a social function they attended together at Lane Hall.

Margaret on her wedding day, June 25, 1946

The hall was constructed in 1916 for the Student Christian Association and the YMCA. By the late 1940s, it was entertaining international student clubs, plays, movies, and dances. Lane Hall also was the place to go for students and faculty members interested in activist causes. Here they could debate whether aid should be given to post-war Europe, the impact of racism on campus, and social reforms such as the 1941 Fair Employment Act, which prohibited racial discrimination by federal agencies, unions, and war-related industry.

A decade earlier, Littell had attended a Nazi Party rally in Nuremberg during a visit to pre-war Germany. He was appalled by what he saw: open racism and antisemitism, and—as the *New York Times* put it—Adolf Hitler's "almost godlike appearance, bathed in a halo of lights." The experience prompted Littell to examine how ancient prejudices dating back to the time of Jesus enabled the murder of six million Jews in the heart of Christian Europe 20 centuries later. Littell later would become known as the father of Holocaust studies.

For now, all eyes were on the happy couple.

Tears welled up in Mae's eyes as Margaret and Marty recited their vows, and she let them flow freely. Mae cried as much from relief as from sadness. She was getting her life and her husband back. But she was losing her daughter once more. Her mind flew back to those horrible days in a Houston hospital room—five years ago, almost to the day—when her daughter had wavered on the very edge of life.

And she worried, too. She knew little of this man who was taking Margaret to his own. How could he possibly care for her as well as she had? Would Margaret be happy? Or would she be miserable, or worse? Mae wanted to go up to the bride and whisper in her ear that she could always come home again. Always. But, of course, Margaret already knew that.

Among the many telegrams and notes of congratulations Margaret received in the days following her wedding was a handwritten letter from the School of Agriculture in Giza, Egypt.

"Here is a word that I would like to whisper to Martin's ears," wrote Dr. Salah Taha, the young man Margaret was dating when she met Marty. "Listen, Martin! You have really selected a real pearl. Everybody will envy you for it, so keep it shining and protect it with everything you own. May God bless your marriage."

The couple stayed in Ann Arbor for a year, so that Margaret could finish her thesis. "He stood over me and made me do it," she joked. Not in an ugly way, of course, but in a supportive, encouraging way. He was upholding his promise to honor her independence. But he was also immensely proud of his new wife. He wanted to see how far she could go.

At the same time, Marty was uncertain about his own career path. What could he do with a doctorate in pharmaceutical chemistry? Margaret suggested teaching. "He was always so good at explaining things," she said years later. "So that's what he went into."

Marty got a job teaching and doing research in the University's Rackham Arthritis Research Unit, one of the first research centers in the country focused on the study of rheumatic diseases. But he also put his feelers out. He wanted to land a job at a big university like Michigan, teaching chemistry. Big, he didn't get. Yet Marty was not dismayed when he received an offer to interview for a faculty position at a mid-sized college in Evansville, Indiana.

Better to be a big fish in a small pond, or so the saying goes.

In June 1947, Margaret completed her thesis. The actual degree would be awarded in August. That summer, after visiting Marty's parents in Newark, the couple moved to Evansville. Marty would start teaching in September at the beginning of the fall term.

And what about Easlick? Had Margaret fulfilled his dream to transform public health through dentistry?

Sadly, that dream has yet to be realized, even 65 years later. General Motors was very good to its original hometown, churning out millions of Buicks and Chevys during the postwar boom. Yet the writing was already on the wall. Even as early as 1940, GM had begun to move its plants into the suburbs. With the plants went the workers and many others—mostly white—who could afford to move. By the late 1960s, an increasingly segregated Flint was challenged by rising rates of unemployment, poverty, and crime, and by a deteriorating infrastructure.

Still, Easlick had much to be grateful for. David had survived the war. For bravery during the Battle of the Bulge, he was awarded the Bronze Star with oak leaf cluster, the Silver Star and—like his father before him—the French Croix de Guerre. David went on to become president of Michigan Bell and Indiana Bell. As vice president of AT&T in the early 1970s, he negotiated an agreement with the U.S. government to implement a historic affirmative action program that enabled women and minorities to move into better-paying jobs.

Breaking barriers. Fulfilling the promise of equal rights, equal health care, and equal opportunity for all Americans.

Those were Margaret's dreams, too.

Chapter Six
Lessons in Courage

Margaret had earned two advanced degrees. But now her main occupation was homemaker, her life defined by the tiny, box-like house Marty had rented for them on South Bennighof Avenue, just two blocks from the Evansville College campus. Homemaker, and perhaps soon, an expectant mother.

Although Margaret shared Marty's strong desire to have a family, she trembled at the prospect. How in the world was she supposed to care for young children when she couldn't feed them, change their diapers, bathe them, or even pick them up and hug them when they cried?

Marty reassured her. He had promised that he would help, and that's what he was going to do. In the fall of 1947, as they were settling into their new home and he was finding his way on campus, Marty and a friend rigged together an artificial arm for her so that she could hold her baby when the time came.

Marty's "Rube Goldberg" invention was a leather and metal harness that draped around Margaret's neck and over her shoulders. The harness was connected to a metal "arm" that fit over the four-inch-long stump on her right side and ended with a hook at the end. Her left side remained "armless" because the two-inch-long stump was too short to fit and operate a prosthetic.

Margaret could, with a slight shrug of her shoulders, operate the arm through an elaborate system of pulleys and gears that made the "elbow" bend.

"It was kinda weird looking," Margaret admitted. The arm was functional, but like the artificial arms that had been crafted for Margaret four years earlier in Minneapolis, it was heavy, uncomfortable, and awkward, and she needed someone to help her get into it.

Margaret didn't dwell on the negative. She never had and never would. What was important was that Marty had cared enough to try. His ungainly contraption was an expression of love.

Around the end of December, after trying to conceive for several months, Margaret missed her period. Her prayers had been answered. She was going to have a baby. Then in April, when she was almost six months along, an event occurred that would change the course of Marty's career and their life together.

The central figure in this drama was a 28-year-old assistant professor of religion and philosophy from Yale University who had arrived on campus in September 1946—the same month as Marty. Boyish looking, with an unruly mop of dark hair and a big, easy smile, George Parker was decidedly liberal when it came to his politics. He supported presidential candidate Henry Wallace who, as leader of the Progressive Party, had mounted a credible challenge to Harry Truman's bid for a second term.

Progressive reformers had done a lot of good for the country in the early years of the 20th Century. Muckrakers and trustbusters, philanthropists, and suffragettes, they included Mother Jones, known as the "most dangerous woman in America" for successfully organizing mineworkers to fight for better wages and working conditions, and Upton Sinclair, whose 1906 expose of the meatpacking industry, *The Jungle*, led to passage of the Pure Food and Drug and Meat Inspection Acts.

But the times, they were a'changin.'

The Soviet Union, an important ally during the war, was now seen as the "Red Menace," intent on extending its tentacles through Europe and even into the United States. In 1947, President Truman enunciated a policy of Soviet containment, the so-called Truman doctrine, which pledged U.S. support of "free peoples who are resisting attempted subjugation." Hearings conducted by the House Un-American Activities Committee showcased allegations that Hollywood was a hotbed of pro-Soviet infiltrators and Communist propaganda. Swept up in redbaiting hysteria, the studios blacklisted more than 300 actors, screenwriters, and directors whose allegiance to their country had been called into question.

These events only stiffened the resolve of Wallace's supporters, Parker among them. Wallace had served under FDR as agriculture secretary and then vice president. A tall, gray-haired man with a reassuring voice, he advocated a host of progressive causes including school desegregation, expansion of the welfare system and national health insurance. What got him into hot water, however, was his support for improving relations with the Soviet Union. A former commerce secretary under Truman, Wallace was forced to resign when he vocally challenged the president's confrontational approach to the Soviets. Now, as candidate for U.S. president, he was regularly vilified by Truman supporters and in the press for being a communist sympathizer and a threat to democracy.

In early April 1948, the Wallace campaign scheduled a speaking engagement in Evansville. The city, a former engine of war-time production, was now known as the "Refrigerator Capitol of the World" for all the kitchen appliances it turned out. Wallace wanted to use it as a backdrop for his proposal to nationalize the military aircraft industry. As chairman of the Vanderburg County Citizens for Wallace, Parker would host the speech, scheduled for April 6 in the city's Memorial Coliseum.

When he heard about it, Evansville College President Lincoln B. Hale called Parker into his office and warned him that his involvement in the Wallace campaign could do serious damage to the college. The president's argument went something like this: Politically conservative local business leaders dominated the board of trustees. They had given a lot of money to the college and would not tolerate left-wing agitators among their faculty. Many of the students were veterans who had fought on the battlefields of Europe and in the jungles of the South Pacific to defend their way of life. They were not about to invite in someone who threatened it.

Parker responded that he didn't want to embarrass the college but could not in good conscience back out of his commitment.

As the date of Wallace's appearance grew closer, enmity between his supporters and opponents intensified. Two days before his speech, the Evansville *Press* published an anti-Wallace editorial entitled "The Big Lie" alongside a political cartoon showing the candidate beating American swords into Soviet sickles.

On the evening of April 6, 500 people came to hear Wallace speak, while outside the Coliseum an unruly crowd four times that size gathered to protest his appearance. As the meeting began, protesters forced their way into the lobby shouting "Communist!" and "Pinkie!" They shattered windows and pounded on the doors of the meeting hall until police were called to disperse the crowd.

Wallace was able to finish his speech without further interruption. But the damage was done. Two days later, the executive committee of the college's board of trustees called for Parker's immediate resignation. The firing created such a furor among the student body, however, that President Hale reinstated him for the remainder of the term after which he would take a "leave" to continue his graduate studies at Yale. Parker never returned to Evansville.

President Hale did something else. He convened a meeting of the faculty in the Student Union Building to discuss the Parker affair. But he was not inviting dissenting opinions. "I want to know," he demanded at one point, "how many of you participated in that riot at the Coliseum. If you were there, please identify yourselves." The room grew quiet. Professors shifted uncomfortably in the rows of folding metal chairs that had been set out for them in the large meeting room. Then one of the chairs scraped across the wooden floor. Marty stood up. President Hale glared at him. Marty glared back, defiantly. After a few silent moments President Hale waved him to sit down and continued with his diatribe. Marty knew his goose was cooked. But he had no regrets.

Meanwhile, 830 miles south in Waco, Texas, Mother's former speech teacher and lifelong friend Sara Lowrey was facing similar challenges. Like Parker, she'd been branded a communist and subversive because she publicly supported Henry Wallace for president. The attacks against Lowrey intensified after she gave a radio address in Houston on July 13, 1948, entitled "Mobilizing for Peace."

"Henry Wallace believes in a firm but fair diplomacy to iron out differences between nations," Lowrey said. "He would have the U.S.A. heavily armed for protection until there could be established an international police force to protect the world ... I agree with Mr. Wallace that we must be militarily stronger than any other nation until we can arm the U. N. and disarm all nations at once. But in the meantime, let us mobilize for peace."

After word of her radio address reached the Baylor campus, angry students splashed red paint on the front door of her house. Her phone rang with hateful messages from anonymous callers. WR White, the Baptist minister who'd succeeded Pat Morris Neff as Baylor president in 1945, did nothing to stop the abuse. Lowrey was a popular and prominent member of the Baylor faculty. White couldn't fire her. But he did everything he could to change her mind about Wallace. Despite the threats and intimidation, Lowrey refused to back down.

On Election Day, third-party candidate Henry Wallace pulled in only about 2% of the popular vote, while—to the surprise of many—Democrat incumbent Harry Truman trounced his Republican rival, Thomas Dewey, to regain the White House. But while tensions on the Baylor campus were dissipating, Lowrey stuck it out for only a few more months before moving to the more hospitable Furman University in Greenville, South Carolina. There she chaired the speech department until her retirement in 1963. During her career, she had co-written a popular textbook on interpretative reading, and at Furman, launched the nation's first televised speech program for children, "How Do You Say It?" She toured widely, speaking at college campuses throughout the country. And she kept up with Margaret. Lowrey beamed with pride to see how far a student of hers had gone.

In a profile published in the *Baylor Line*, a university publication, in 1972, Dorothy Hanson, a member of the Baylor faculty who knew Lowrey during the hard years, summed up her colleague's inner strengths—"intellectual integrity, absolute honesty, remarkable courage to state her convictions even under pressure to do otherwise, and a great will to give herself for the good of others." That, Hanson said, was the secret of the profound effect Lowrey had on those around her. Sara Lowrey died in 1991 at the age of 93.

While the flames of anti-Communist fervor were being fanned throughout the country, Margaret focused on her pregnancy. On August 7, 1948, she delivered a healthy baby boy. He was named Philip, after Marty's father.

At this point in Margaret's story, she has a new narrator—me, her firstborn son. From here on out, she will be called Mother, of course. For now, she is more than a single person, more than a wife. Her life from this point forward is more than hers alone. One day she will put her dental degree to use. But even when the sign on her door announces "Margaret Chanin, DDS," and she signs her letters with "Dr." in front her name, she will also wear another title proudly: "Margaret Chanin, Mother."

The first few weeks after the birth of a baby are intense for any parent, but for my mother, they were as challenging as anything she had experienced since the accident. Whenever I cried, Dad—or somebody—had to be there to pick me up and attend to my needs. Dad cradled me in his arms while I nursed. He changed my diapers, bathed me, rocked me in his arms to console me and nestled me in my crib. In short, he did everything a mother would do except provide the milk.

Still, Mother worried. How could she get me out of the house should there be a fire while Dad was away teaching night classes? "I finally decided that if worse came to worst, I could always jerk up the four corners of the crib sheet and carry him outside in my teeth," she told a reporter years later.

That was not a satisfactory solution, of course. After a few days, my parents hired a nanny, a Black woman named Mabel, so Dad could go back to work. Domestic service was one of the few jobs open to Black women at that time. I don't know Mabel's last name, or how long she worked for us. But she made it possible for Mother to care for an infant and run the household. While Mabel looked after me, Mother would take the bus to market and return with the large pockets of her coat brimming with canned goods, bottles of milk, fresh vegetables, and fruit. Dad often referred to his resourceful wife as a "Bala Bosteh," a Yiddish term which, loosely translated, means "a woman with a well-stocked pantry."

For Mother loved to cook. Even with a new baby in tow, she made sure a homecooked meal was ready and waiting when Dad walked through the front door at the end of his day. How? She clenched her teeth—literally. She'd nestle an egg from the refrigerator between her chin and her shoulder, lean over, and crack it on the side of the skillet, and scramble it with a spatula gripped between her teeth. If she were baking, she'd sip about a teaspoon's amount of vanilla into a straw, walk over to the mixing bowl, and release her tongue from the tip of the straw, allowing the vanilla to flow into the bowl.

Of course, Dad helped make that happen. In every house we lived in, he installed modified door handles and floor switches so she could turn the lights on or off with her foot. He retrofitted the kitchen with a special stove and oven, so she could adjust the temperature setting and move pots and pans around with her prosthesis, and he installed spring-action latches on the drawers so she could open them with her big toe.

"I was Marty's Pygmalion, you know," Mother confessed to an interviewer in 1997, referring to the George Bernard Shaw play about a British professor of phonetics who transforms a Cockney flower girl into a lady. "He was determined to give me independence and do all those things to make me independent. I'm able to do a lot of things I would never have done had it not been for Marty.

"He was kind of a controlling person, but maybe I might have needed that. He pushed me so. He was so determined that I keep my figure that he never let me leave the bedroom in the morning until I had gotten down on the floor. He held my shoulders while I raised my feet and then held my feet while I raised my shoulders. I told him, 'You never said anything about me being too heavy when we were going together,' and he said, 'Well, I wasn't too sure of you then.'"

These first years in Evansville were happy ones for my parents. They certainly made an impression on Gordon "Bish" Thompson, a columnist for the *Evansville Press*, who penned this remembrance of them:

"They sat together at a table near ours at Smitty's. We noticed them because they were having such a good time together. Their conversation was animated and must have been on a highly jocular level because they laughed together over remarks they alone could hear. It struck me that there was something unusual about this man and woman, but it took several minutes of casual observance before I could figure out what it was. He was feeding her every bite she ate. It was done so naturally it's no wonder most people about them didn't even notice it. They finished their meal, dawdled, and visited over their coffee – the man sipping his and then holding her cup to her lips – and left. At the door he put her coat over her shoulders and out they went. I doubt if more than a half-dozen people who saw them at dinner that evening realized the woman had no arms ...

Marty and Margaret attend the Pi Kappa fraternity spring formal, April 1949

"In the months that followed there were many more times when I'd hear someone tell of seeing Mrs. Chanin about our city. Most of them didn't know her name. They had happened to notice that when she got on the bus, she'd ask the driver to take the fare from her cloak. She had big pockets on either side. Or someone would tell me about seeing her shopping downtown. Clerks would be asked to take money from her pocket, replace the change with the sales slip, put the smaller purchases in the other pocket and send the larger ones out to the house by parcel delivery."

"This I couldn't help but notice: Everyone who mentioned seeing Mrs. Chanin would report the incident with frank admiration. Some marveled at the normal way she handled an abnormal situation. Most people remarked about her courage ... Is that courage, to pick up the pieces after your life has been dealt a blow like that? Is (it) something special that is mysteriously provided to those who will need it? Or is it lying somewhere inside most of us, to serve us if misfortune puts the arm on our shoulders?

"The few years the Chanins were here gave Evansville a dramatic and impressive lesson in human courage. We are the richer for it. But if you are like I, your admiration is not at all backed up by the confidence you could do it, too, should you one day lose both your arms. The experts in these matters say we could. But I don't know."

Dad made his own impression. He plunged into college life, accompanying chemistry students on a trip to Chicago to attend the American Chemical Society convention, and serving as faculty advisor for the Camera Club. Photography was a passion of his. Dad arranged for a dark room to be set up in the physics laboratory. Using equipment loaned by members of the group, he provided instruction in developing and printing, and showed students how to take portraits and action photos.

Still, Dad could not let go of the assault on academic freedom he'd witnessed. In April 1949, seven months after Truman's reelection, the Evansville College Speakers Bureau published its annual bulletin, listing the expertise of more than 50 faculty members who were available to speak to community groups and organizations. Curiously, Dad's expertise was listed not as chemistry but as "International Control of Atomic Energy," a reference to a 1946 report by an advisory committee to the president that advocated international control of nuclear weapons and avoidance of future nuclear warfare. The high-minded plan was shelved when the Soviets refused U.S. demands that they agree never to develop a bomb. On August 29, 1949, the Soviets conducted their first nuclear test. The "Cold War" had just become a little hotter.

It is a testament to the complexity of the human character that Dad was a thorn in the side of the college's administration while simultaneously being one of the most popular professors on campus and in the community. He drew accolades for his volunteer work in the special education class at the Wheeler School in Evansville, where he fixed and constructed equipment and chairs for children with physical disabilities. He would continue to design and build supportive equipment for people with disabilities throughout his life.

In November 1949, around the time of the college's Homecoming celebration, Dad also won the "Ugly Man" Contest. Students paid for the right to cast a ballot in the contest, which was sponsored by the Alpha Phi Omega service fraternity. Proceeds went to buy Thanksgiving baskets for needy families. According to *The Crescent*, the student newspaper, "Professor Chanin is a remarkable individual" who now could boast honorary membership in the fraternity as a result of his "singular position."

College leaders did not share *The Crescent*'s assessment. Dad certainly was popular among the students but as far as the administration was concerned, he was uncooperative and argumentative. To his chairman, Dr. Alvin Strickler, a law-and-order guy who had founded and directed the Evansville Police Department's first training school in the 1930s, Dad had an oversized ego. He was not a team player. President Hale also had not forgotten Dad's moment of defiance during the faculty meeting two years before. And so, around the New Year, Dad was notified that his contract would not be renewed for the 1950-1951 school year. He would be allowed to finish out the spring term but then it would be announced he was approved for a "leave," the same end-of-the-road George Parker had accepted in 1948.

This news would have been bad enough. But around the same time, Mother discovered that she was expecting again. She broke down in tears. How could she take care of a new baby, a toddler, and now an out-of-work husband?

Mother and Dad packed up and we moved in with her folks on the farm back in Arkansas. We had nowhere else to go.

Chapter Seven
City of Angels, City of Hope

Of course, my grandparents were delighted to have their daughter back home, and to spend time with their grandson, if even for a short time. For Dad had his feelers out to his network of friends back in Michigan. His job search became more frantic in June, when Communist North Korea invaded U.S.-backed South Korea. In August, Congress appropriated $12 billion for military action in Korea, and reinstated the draft. Men who had served in World War II were exempted.

Robert "Bob" Chanin was born August 15, 1950, in a Memphis hospital, the closest to Osceola. He was named for Mother's father. For the second time in nine years, Dad's obligation to serve in the armed forces was deferred, for now he was the father of two children. He also had a job that was important to the war effort. He'd just accepted a position as a professor of chemistry in the College of Pharmacy at the Detroit Institute of Technology.

Bob was just a week old when Dad went back to Michigan to find a new home for his family. Mother had plenty of help from Grandmother, who was always there when her daughter needed her. But that would soon end, and Mother would have to set up a new household 700 miles away, by herself. Old feelings of dread flooded back. How was she ever to manage?

By now Dad had decided not to resettle the family in downtown Detroit. As had happened in Flint, the auto plants had long since moved to the suburbs, leaving behind communities with few jobs, declining schools and streets littered with trash. Instead, he went back to Ann Arbor and found a house on South Fifth Avenue in a pleasant, leafy neighborhood, blocks from the University of Michigan's South Quadrangle, a new men's dormitory. From here he could take the Penn Central commuter train and be in the classroom in Detroit in a little over an hour.

Dad called Mother from the home of a friend of my parents in Ann Arbor. "I found a house," he said. "We can get it if we give a larger-than-normal down payment."

"How much?" Mother asked.

"$5,000."

Mother asked if the basement leaked. At that point their friend got on the line.

"Oh, Margaret," she said, "it's been raining for five days, and the basement's as dry as a bone."

The next day Mother went to the bank, cashed five $1,000 government bonds and wired Dad the money. Six weeks later, in mid-October, the rest of the Chanin clan took the train to Ann Arbor—which even today takes the better part of 24 hours. On board was an armless woman, a 2-year-old toddler, a baby in a basket, and the woman's gray-haired mother. Grandmother helped with the move and stayed with us for nearly a month until Mother got settled. A couple of days before Thanksgiving, Grandmother went home to Osceola so she could spend the holiday with her husband.

Mother was on her own again. She received a few responses to an ad she placed in the *Detroit Free Press* for a housekeeper, "white or colored," private room and bath included. While she was usually able to find someone to help her, sometimes the help didn't stay. Once, when she was nursing Bob, the woman she'd hired suddenly quit and left her alone with a baby and a toddler. Bob was crying, hungry, and helpless in his crib. Somehow Mother struggled out of her blouse, leaned over the crib, and maneuvered a nipple into Bob's mouth so he could nurse until Dad came home from work.

Dad would catch the 6:20 a.m. train in the morning and not get home until 6:30 p.m. at night. Mother was never able to find help willing to work past 5 p.m. That meant Dad would have to swing into action as soon as he walked through our front door. He'd help get dinner on the table, bathe me and my brother, and read to us, and get us to bed by 9 or 9:30 p.m. Then, in the winter, he'd have to go out and shovel snow. If he didn't keep the front steps and walk down to the street free of snow, the postman wouldn't deliver the mail. It was a city ordinance.

One morning in January, Mother couldn't wake Dad up. She called the college and said he wouldn't be coming in; he was ill. When he finally awoke in the afternoon, she made him go to the doctor, who told him he was suffering from "sheer exhaustion." This happened every winter.

Despite the spotty help and Dad being around only in the evenings and on weekends, I never heard Mother complain or express resentment about her lot in life. If she thought at all about the career she'd put on hold, it was only during those rare, brief breaths of quiet and calm granted women who are in the thick of childrearing. In later years, when asked how she ever was able to care for not one, but two young children, she'd quip, "Well, fools rush in where angels fear to tread. If I had tried to work it all out, I would have never had one."

Then she'd add, "I happen to be in the position that when I try to do something, be it opening a can or whatever, the more I can't do it, the more determined I am to do it. I get so mad. I am not going to be defeated by this thing."

Our mother of invention figured out early that her children could help, too. "When they were real small," Grandmother recalled years later, "she would lean over their cribs and tell them over and over to put their arms around her neck. They soon learned and she could lift them up."

When Bob and I reached our third birthdays, Mother put us to work, making our beds, emptying the wastebaskets in our rooms—even dusting the dining room furniture. As I grew older, I was put in charge of ironing. She'd pay me a penny for each handkerchief I ironed, five cents for a pillowcase. Bob and I had to help with the household chores. There was no alternative.

Years later when I was on my own, she'd laugh when I'd say, "All boys ought to have armless mothers until they're grown." She agreed. At least in my generation, girls had to learn how to cook and keep house, while boys generally were let off the hook when it came to doing chores at home. "There shouldn't be any such thing as man's work or woman's work," Mother would say. "It's work. Getting it done gets it done."

Despite his constant fatigue, especially during the winter, Dad loved his job and had good relationships with his colleagues and Dr. Curtis H. Waldon, dean of the College of Pharmacy. Nevertheless, he was acutely aware that the artificial arm he'd made for Mother in Evansville was not working well for her. The skin of the stump of her right arm was inflamed from the friction and pressure of her prosthesis. Something must be done about this. But he had no idea what to do.

Then, in early 1952, Mother got a phone call.

"Is this Dr. Margaret Chanin?" the man's voice on the line asked.

"Yes, who is this?"

"I'm Eugene Murphy. I'm assistant director of the Prosthetic and Sensory Aids Service at the Veterans Administration in New York City. I was attending a meeting in Chicago this week when I heard about you from one of your husband's classmates at Michigan. He said your husband built you a prosthetic arm. Do you mind if I come over to see it?"

What a strange request. Mother hesitated, assuming this was some sort of prank or worse. But something told her to hold on a minute.

"Why do you want to do that?" she asked.

"I'm interested," Dr. Murphy said, "and I think I can help you. There have been a lot of advances in artificial limbs just in the past five years."

"Ah, OK," Mother said, still a bit skeptical. "When would you like to drop by?"

"How about now?" he responded. "I'm on campus. I drove in from Chicago this morning."

"All right, but could you give me 20 minutes?"

Precisely 20 minutes later, there was a knock at the door. On the doorstep stood a slightly stooped middle-aged man in a suit and tie with a cane in each hand. He smiled.

"Hi, I'm Dr. Murphy."

"Oh," Mother said, surprised. "Won't you come in?"

Murphy looked up at her and smiled mischievously.

"You were expecting Dr. Kildare?" he asked.

They both laughed, breaking the ice. Mother directed her guest to the couch in the living room. Before they got down to the purpose of his visit, and at Mother's request, he told her his story.

Eugene Murphy was born in Syracuse, New York, in 1913. When he was 11, he contracted polio. The virus attacked the nerves, paralyzing his legs. In the 1920s, little could be done for victims of this disease, which was spread from person to person and through infected food and water.

Eugene's parents read about an amazing therapy. The waters of a resort in Warm Springs, Georgia, had helped a well-known New York politician, Franklin Delano Roosevelt, whose legs had been paralyzed by polio in 1921 when he was 39. On a friend's recommendation, FDR went down to Georgia in 1924 and took a swim in the therapeutic waters and immediately felt an improvement. For the first time in three years, he could move his right leg. While not a cure, FDR's experience attracted national publicity. And that's how Eugene ended up in Warm Springs, swimming with the future New York governor and future president of the United States. After a year of therapy, Eugene was able to leave his wheelchair and walk with the help of crutches.

Mother looked concerned. Murphy nodded grimly. Outbreaks of polio terrorized communities across the country every summer. "Don't worry," he said softly. "I'm not infectious. And there is hope. I hear they're working on a vaccine."

"You said you were a doctor?" Mother asked.

"Oh, that," he said modestly. "I have a PhD in mechanical engineering. Started out at Ingersoll Rand, making industrial compressors. But then decided I wanted to help people like you. But enough about me. Now I want to see that amazing artificial arm I've heard so much about. I see that you're not wearing it."

Mother stood up, bent over a side table next to the couch and pulled off the cloth napkin that covered it with her teeth. Underneath was the leather and metal contraption that Marty and his friend had made for her.

Murphy gasped. "Would it be OK if I helped you put it on so I can see how it works?" he asked.

Mother nodded. Murphy struggled to his feet, and then helped slip the harness over her neck and shoulders so that it held the prosthesis in place over the right stump. She showed him how she could maneuver the limb with a shrug of her shoulder.

"This is amazing," he marveled. "It looks like it was made by a prisoner-of-war who had heard that there was such a thing as an artificial arm but had never seen one!"

"He meant well," Mother said. "I just can't wear it very long before it starts hurting."

"There's a school starting in Los Angeles, at UCLA and the VA," he responded. "They're looking for 'experimental amputees' to help them design better prosthetics. I believe they could design a better arm for you."

Murphy thanked Mother for allowing him to stop by on such short notice and headed toward the door. "Thank you, Margaret," he said. "It's been a real pleasure."

"Thank you, Dr. Murphy," she responded. "You are the answer to many prayers."

When Dad got home from work that evening, Mother told him about the visit she'd had and about the opportunity to go to UCLA. But she told him she didn't want to go, because Marty would have to find another job and they'd have to move to a strange city with two young children in tow. It was too much trouble.

"Margaret," he responded firmly, "I'll dig ditches if I have to, to make you independent."

It had seemed too good to be true, like a dream that hovers in the fuzzy margin between sleep and wake and then dissolves in the light of day.

She'd had the same dream many times. She was whole again. She could feed and dress herself and comb her hair. Most important, she could wrap her two precious little boys in her arms and hold them tight. She would often awaken from this dream choking a sob, hot tears stinging her cheeks, sobs and tears she could not stifle or wipe away without burying her face in her pillow.

Now here she was, on a brilliant summer day, in the front seat of a brand new, 1953 Ford station wagon. With her husband at the wheel, and her boys in the backseat, she was cruising Wilshire Boulevard in downtown Los Angeles, what was known as the "Miracle Mile."

Sobs gathered at the back of her throat; tears welled up in her blue eyes. She stifled them. She didn't want the children to see her cry, so she tried to divert their attention.

"Look at that!"

"Where?" Bob and I answered, almost in unison.

"There!" Mother shouted, tilting her head at the curved fronts of the art deco buildings in front of them.

Buildings made entirely of highly polished glass and soft, honey-colored stone. Streets choked with traffic and lined with palm trees. Wide sidewalks bustling with shoppers, many clutching bags emblazoned with department store logos: Desmond's, Coulter's, the May Co. It all seemed so unreal, like a fairy tale.

Mother shook her head to dislodge the notion. This was no dream. But it was indeed a miracle. What she was experiencing now was the answer to an oft-repeated prayer. Her arms had not magically reappeared, but she was whole.

The tears rose again. This time she let them spill freely.

"What's the matter, Mommy?" I asked. Even at 5 years old, I was ever the Observant One. "Why are you sad?"

"I'm not sad," she replied, with as much cheerfulness as she could muster. "I've never been happier."

She looked over at Dad and smiled gratefully. Without taking his eyes from the road ahead, he put his hand on her knee, and kept it there.

For Dad had enthusiastically encouraged her to apply to the new school at the UCLA Prosthesis Training Center. It was he who had gathered the material for her application to be an amputee subject in a school for doctors, physical therapists, and prosthetists from around the country. It was he who had sent the photos of her wearing the rudimentary artificial limb he'd made for her. Funded by the VA, the aim of the program was to develop, fit, and provide the latest in artificial limb technology to veteran amputees and others who had lost limbs.

And when her application was accepted, Dad found a good job doing research at the City of Hope National Medical Center in Duarte, and a house on Rochester Avenue close to the UCLA campus. As soon as he could, he packed us up and moved us out to California.

City of Angels, City of Hope. The next chapter of Mother's life had begun.

Chapter Eight
A Rare Case

The Prosthetics Training Center was a joint effort of the UCLA College of Engineering and School of Medicine. Supported by the U.S. Veterans Administration and endorsed by the National Academy of Sciences-National Research Council's Advisory Committee on Artificial Limbs, the UCLA center was part of a nationwide effort to meet the demand for the latest in prosthetics materials and technology by veteran amputees and others who had lost their limbs.

The double hook, which could be opened and closed at the end of an upper extremity prosthetic, had been around since the early part of the century—invented by D.W. Dorrance, who'd lost his right arm in a lumber mill accident in 1906. But development of functional prosthetic arms would have to wait for the innovations that came out of the of the aviation industry during World War II.

An unlikely wartime partnership between an orthopedic surgeon, Dr. John Lotzenheiser, and a pioneering aircraft designer and industrialist, John K. "Jack" Northrop, led to two key developments: a sturdy and lightweight plastic laminate for making sockets and arm shells, and use of the Bowden cable, a flexible steel wire cable used in airplanes and automobiles, which made it much easier for amputees to operate their artificial arms.

UCLA's role in the development of prosthetics began in 1946 with the arrival of Craig Lee Taylor, PhD, an Army Air Corps veteran with a doctorate in physiology from Stanford University. Under his leadership as professor of Engineering and Physiology, the UCLA College of Engineering developed one of the nation's first comprehensive programs in biotechnology and biomechanics.

It had been long recognized that through "biscapular abduction," the tensing of various muscles of their backs and shoulders, amputees could be taught how to convert muscle power into the mechanical motion needed to operate their artificial arms. In a similar way, the squeezing of a bicycle brake handle pulls on a cable that closes the brake pads over the wheel rims. Taylor refined this understanding through time-and-motion analyses of normal arms. As journalist Bess Furman put it in a 1962 government progress report on prosthetics, "He figured out precisely what was needed in the mechanism controlling a prosthesis in order to perform (its) function with a minimum of effort."

By the early 1950s the U.S. government, especially the VA, had spent millions of dollars on research to develop better artificial arms. The problem now was getting them to the veteran amputees who needed them. As Dr. Miles H. Anderson, director of UCLA's Prosthetics Education Program, noted in a 1961 review article, "The techniques and knowledge needed to successfully fabricate and fit these new arms of plastic, with their strange harnessing and power transmission systems, were too complex to be mastered by merely reading a report or seeing a demonstration."

Doctors and physical therapists knew nothing about these new prostheses and so could not prescribe them or train amputees how to use them. Hundreds of veterans who had lost their arms in the war were going without.

Thus emerged the concept of a school where physicians, therapists, and prosthetists would be taught how to fit the new arms and train amputees how to use them. UCLA, where many of the improvements in upper extremity prosthetics had been pioneered, was chosen to set up the first Prosthetics Training Center. The program partnered initially with Northrop Aviation, a few miles south in Hawthorne, to fabricate the limbs, and later, with the Sierra Engineering Company in Sierra Madre, just east of Pasadena, on the design and manufacture of the components.

Based in the College of Engineering's Mechanics Building Annex across Westwood Boulevard from the football field, the first six-week "school" opened on January 1, 1953. Within two years, hundreds of physicians, therapists, and prosthetists had taken knowledge gained at UCLA to prosthetic clinics and rehabilitation facilities across the country. The impact was profound. A case could be made, Anderson concluded, that the cost of education, research, and training in the new artificial arms was recouped many times over through income taxes collected from amputees who found good-paying jobs on account of their improved prostheses.

Mother arrived in time for the fourth session of UCLA's prosthetic training school that began in September 1953. She and the other amputees who participated volunteered to be case subjects for the students. They were examined, tested, and questioned by the physicians and surgeons who prepared prescriptions for the type of limb to be made by the prosthetists. The prosthetists, in turn, conducted their own examinations, testing, and questioning, as they fitted their artificial limbs onto the stumps of the amputee volunteers. And finally, more testing and questioning from the physical therapists, who tested various training protocols to help the amputees achieve the highest functional use of their new limbs.

Over the course of six "schools," from early September 1953 to the middle of August 1954, 12 different arms—six for the right and six for the left—had been prescribed for Mother by a series of physicians, fabricated for her, and fitted to her by several different prosthetists, and she had been trained to use them by a succession of physical therapists.

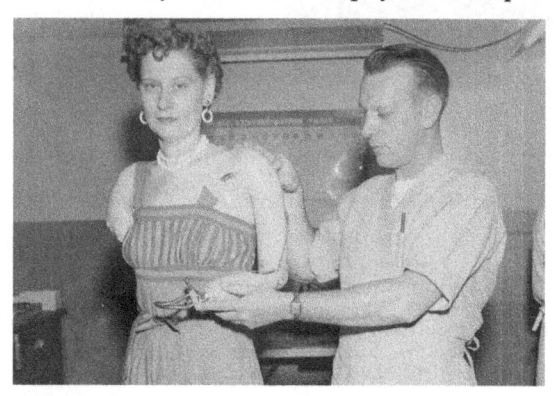

A UCLA prosthetist helps Mother during a "fitting."

The repetitive process could easily have been frustrating and exhausting, but Mother, for the most part, felt exhilarated and liberated. She had learned in the early days after her accident that it would not help her to be shy or embarrassed about her condition. Now she exposed her stumps for examination by dozens of strangers, mostly men, without a touch of nervousness or shame. On the contrary, she felt excited—even proud—because she was helping them. She was teaching them. They were learning from her how to help other amputees. And in the process, she hoped that she would end up with a prosthesis that was easier for her to put on by herself, which she could wear for long periods without discomfort, and which, most importantly, would open new doors of independence for her.

Indeed, Dr. Charles O. Bechtol, a surgeon from Yale University and consultant to the VA who flew frequently to the West Coast to oversee the training of the physicians and surgeons in the UCLA program, told a Los Angeles newspaper that Mother not only presented them with a complex case, but she "became an excellent teacher of the practical problems facing women amputees. Many women amputees will benefit from her work."

When time allowed, Mother visited amputees who were recovering from their operations in local VA hospitals. She was a housewife, too, and the mother of two young boys. Somehow, despite the demands of her schedule at the training center, she made time to keep house, go to the market, and prepare the meals. She participated in our school through the PTA and made sure we attended church regularly with her. And of course, she applied a liberal dose of motherly guidance.

Mother and her boys, Philip and Robert. Portrait by Wilbur Curtis for the Memphis Press-Scimitar, 1957

"Dinnertime is an awfully good opportunity to get in teaching that I want to get across to the boys," she told an interviewer at one point. "Since I have to be fed, I am free to talk, read bits from correspondence and other things of family interest, and thus take advantage of my 'captive audience.'"

Mother had help—a woman hired to come in regularly to help with the house cleaning, and to dress and take her to campus when Dad couldn't because of his work schedule. But increasingly I was helping her, too. By the age of 5, I had learned how to open cans in the kitchen, take food out of the oven, and help with other mealtime and household chores. "I got to wondering whether I was expecting too much of a 5-year-old," Mother told a reporter in 1967, "and I asked a schoolteacher about it. She said, 'No, most people don't realize the full potentialities of a 5-year-old child.' She said I should let him do as much as he can, that it was good for children to accept as much responsibility as they can."

Occasionally, and especially when Bob began to take on more responsibility as he grew older, we'd complain that our friends didn't have to do household chores like we did. Even before the griping had popped out of our mouths, however, we knew how Mother would respond.

"Well," she'd always say, "the other kids don't have an armless mother."

It wasn't all work. "We played board games as a family," Bob recalled years later, "and did not watch TV. We had pets and projects and activities and were especially encouraged to read and talk and think."

Dad seemed to be having as much fun we were. On the weekends, he'd take us on excursions to explore our strange new world: the La Brea Tar Pits, which displayed the excavated bones of woolly mammoths and saber-toothed tigers that walked the earth 10,000 years ago; the Griffith Park observatory and zoo; and the Pike amusement zone in Long Beach, which boasted a wooden roller coaster dubbed "the World's Greatest Ride."

Dad also was excelling in his position as pharmaceutical chemist at the City of Hope, a former tuberculosis sanitarium that would become renowned for its cancer research and treatment programs. Dad worked in the thoracic research laboratory of Dr. Alfred Goldman, chief of Thoracic and Cardiac Surgery. In May 1954, the local paper in nearby Monrovia, the *Daily News-Post*, reported that Dad had developed a faster and more sensitive

Portrait of Marty by Hungarian-born artist János Bernát

method for measuring the blood chloride level. This is an essential prerequisite for surgery, as an abnormal chloride level may indicate kidney problems that could lead to complications during and after the operation. Dad also was excelling in his position as pharmaceutical chemist at the City of Hope. It was here that he met János Bernát, a Hungarian-born artist who was being treated for lung cancer. Known for his Biblical-themed portraits and murals, Bernát, who died in 1964, gave his friend a charcoal drawing that Mother would preserve carefully in her scrapbooks.

In August 1954, about the time she finished her fourth six-week school session, Mother was chosen for an experimental surgery program at St. John's Hospital in Santa Monica. Developed by Drs. Bechtol and Taylor, the program aimed to increase the success of the fitting and functioning of artificial limbs.

An international leader in biomechanics and the design of orthopedic device systems and artificial limbs, Dr. Bechtol would go on to establish the Division of Orthopedic Surgery at UCLA. With Dr. Taylor, he also advanced the field of cineplasty, the surgical isolation of a loop of muscle in the chest or arm for attachment of a prosthetic device. Amputees learned to operate their device by contracting the loop muscle.

According to a story about her published in April 1955 in the *Santa Monica Outlook*, Mother was selected for this new type of surgery, "a rare case in medical history," because through her previous background as a dentist she had achieved a high degree of brain-muscle coordination and dexterity.

Of course, Mother had had only two years of training as a dentist before she lost her arms. Equally important to her selection as an experimental surgery subject, perhaps, was her previous athleticism. She had been an excellent swimmer before the accident and continued to tone her body, including her back and shoulder muscles, in the pool even now. Mother had other qualities that no doubt impressed Bechtol – an unflappable, sunny disposition combined with a fierce determination to succeed. Interviewed midway through a course of several operations, she told the reporter that while she realized she would never resume her career as a dentist, there were "scores" of useful endeavors at which she could become proficient. "With my present studies and further surgery," she said, "I shall master what I attempt."

And what of Eugene Murphy, who led Mother to UCLA in the first place?

He went on to direct the VA's Research Center for Prosthetics. From 1973 until his retirement in 1983, he served as director of Technology Transfer, overseeing and expediting projects, fostering collaborations, and mentoring young people who also would become key figures in rehabilitation research and development. "Dr. Murphy's efforts, as author and technical consultant, are largely responsible for major texts published in the prosthetic field," the Syracuse, New York, newspaper proclaimed of its native son in 1961, the year he was honored by the President's Committee on Employment of the Physically Handicapped.

Eugene Murphy died in Ithaca, New York, in 2000. He was 87.

"The patient was an unusually intelligent, normally developed woman who was well adjusted to her handicap. The only abnormality was in the loss of her arms."

Thus began the report of a daring operation to solve a long-standing problem for Mother—the inability to fit her with a left-arm prosthesis because her stump was too short. Attempting the procedure at St. John's Hospital in Santa Monica would be Drs. Marshall R. Urist and Robert Mazet Jr., orthopedic surgeons at UCLA who had honed their skills on the battlefields of World War II.

Urist served with the U.S. Army Medical Corps in Europe and was particularly skilled in the repair of open hip fractures. He was best known for his discovery in 1965 of bone morphogenetic protein (BMP), a genetically produced "bone glue" that helps bone regenerate. Urist proved that BMP could stimulate the growth of living bone tissue around surgical pins and screws used to repair broken hips, shoulders, and other bones.

As a captain in the U.S. Navy 3rd Amphibious Corps Medical Battalion, Mazet was awarded the Bronze Star and Navy Commendation Medal for valor during the Battle of Okinawa, one of the bloodiest battles in the Pacific. After the war, he was appointed chief of Orthopedic Surgery at the Wadsworth Veterans Administration Hospital in Los Angeles, where he pioneered the development of prosthetic and orthotic devices.

In their initial evaluation, Urist and Mazet noted a large, sagging mass of fatty tissue and skin hanging from the stump of Mother's right arm, which had been amputated about five inches below the shoulder. The skin was inflamed from the friction and pressure of her prosthesis. The soft parts were tender and contained what was presumed to be a neuroma, a benign but painful growth from the median nerve, which normally supplies the forearm muscles. The object of their inquiry, her left arm, had been amputated about three inches below the shoulder. Although Mother could revolve the head of the upper arm freely on all sides, a mass of skin, fat, and scar tissue hung down two to three inches below the end of the bone and was an obstacle to fitting a socket for an artificial limb.

On September 10, 1954, Mother underwent a first operation to remove the neuroma and a bone spur from the right stump. Eight days later came a more extensive, second procedure—an attempt to lengthen the left stump by taking a four-inch piece of her fibula, a non-weight bearing bone in the calf next to the shin bone and grafting it into a channel that had been drilled into the upper arm bone of the stump. The bone graft was covered by a sack of skin, fatty and fibrous tissue, and atrophied muscle sewn together with black silk sutures.

"This was a long ordeal," Mother recalled.

It took three weeks for the stump to heal, and three months before she could walk on her right leg without pain. In November, two months after the operation, a prosthesis was fitted over the left stump, but it became painful after a few minutes of use. By January 1955, the skin had become ulcerated, so in February, Mother underwent a third operation to repair the skin and to remove enough of the bone graft—about four tenths of an inch—to allow the soft parts to move more freely over the end of the bone. The stump healed slowly. After six weeks, in early spring, Margaret was refitted with the prosthesis, but the stump remained swollen, tender, and still quite painful.

Meanwhile, the right stump had healed nicely. Mother was fitted with a new prosthesis. She took the arm home and found that—for the first time—she could put it on and take it off by herself by lying on her back on the bed. Her new limb was also five ounces lighter, with an aluminum hook on the end instead of a stainless steel one. Without the sagging mass of skin and fatty tissue and the painful neuroma, it was more comfortable and worked better than any prosthesis she had ever had. "I felt like getting down on my knees and thanking the Lord," she told an interviewer in 1997.

As she adjusted to the prosthesis, Mother's cooking skills improved. She was able to put a cake pan in the oven without spilling any of the batter. She could operate household appliances, including the vacuum cleaner. With a "spork," a combination spoon-and-fork that fit on the end of the prosthesis, she could bring food to her mouth on her own for the first time since the accident. Feeding herself with the spork was so exhausting and time-consuming, however, that she rarely used it after she left the program.

That didn't matter so much. More important, with the help of the UCLA physical therapists and prosthetists working together, for the first time in her life, Mother learned to drive a car.

Chapter Nine
The Best Driver

On a bright summer day in June 1955, Dad took the day off and drove Mother to the Prosthesis Training Center. They were met in the parking lot by a therapist named Roger and a "test car" to which the UCLA wizards had made a few adjustments. A button underneath the door handle popped open the door on the driver's side. A plastic ring mounted onto the steering wheel enabled Mother to turn the wheel with the hook of her artificial arm. And an extension to the gearshift on the steering column made it possible for her to shift gears using her left leg.

"Ready to take 'er for a spin?" Roger asked.

Mother laughed and shook her head. Impossible. He was asking her to do the impossible. At that moment, she pictured Dean Elliott at the bedside of a disfigured young woman in deep despair, telling her that, yes, she would become a dentist. Mother took a deep breath and slid behind the steering wheel. Roger went around to the passenger side, and Dad squeezed into the backseat. The starter, and horn and turn signal had all been moved to the floorboard. Roger showed her how to operate them by pressing each button with her foot.

"OK," he said. "Let's go."

Mother stepped on the starter and the engine roared to life.

"Hurrah!" Dad shouted from the backseat.

Mother giggled like a schoolgirl.

"Very good," Roger said. "Now, before you take us for a ride, show us how you're going to steer this boat on wheels."

Mother raised the artificial arm. It took a couple of minutes before she could maneuver the hook into the ring on the steering wheel. But once in, she could move the wheel back and forth.

"You know where the brake is?" Roger asked.

Mother pressed her right foot onto the brake pedal.

"Fine," he said. "Now this may be a little tricky, but you're going to have to pull the gear shift to the left to get it out of gear, then push it up for drive or down for reverse."

With her right foot still firmly on the brake, Mother pressed her left leg against the gear shift extender. Eventually she was able to pop the gear shift out of neutral and push it into drive. The transmission responded accordingly.

"Nicely done," Roger said.

He paused, took a long look at his pupil, then broke out in another big smile.

"OK, hot shot," he said. "Let's drive."

Mother locked the hook into the ring on the steering wheel and looked intently ahead. She could feel her shoulders and jaw tensing. Her first driving lesson was in the near-empty parking lot at the School of Engineering, not an actual road, but to her it seemed like she was merging onto Wilshire Boulevard at rush hour.

She took a deep breath and pressed down on the accelerator with her right foot. The car lunged forward, surprising her. She hit the brake and the car stopped short. She'd gone about four feet.

"That's it," Roger reassured her. "Nice and easy."

This time, Mother eased her foot onto the accelerator. The car ambled forward. She looked down at the speedometer. She was only going about 10 miles an hour, but that was fast enough for now.

"OK," he said, "now turn left."

Mother pulled instead of pushed, however, and the car took off toward the right. Momentarily flummoxed, she hit the brake again. "Dang it!" she exclaimed, uttering a rare but sanitized version of the expletive that was a favorite of her father's.

The men in the car burst out laughing. She didn't mind. She knew they weren't laughing at her. Anyone watching was probably having a good laugh, too. The Three Stooges take a driving lesson—only one of them is a woman without arms.

By the end of her hour-long lesson, Mother was giving her two passengers a smooth ride, gliding in circles, right and left. Stopping and backing up. Pulling into a parking space.

"Margaret, you were wonderful!" Dad exclaimed as she turned off the engine and removed the key from the ignition. "I'm so proud of you!"

"Not bad for a first lesson," Roger agreed. "Next time we'll try parallel parking."

"And then can I drive downtown?" Mother asked.

Roger's eyes widened. "Whenever you feel you're ready to handle it, Mrs. Chanin."

"Oh, she can handle it," Dad interjected. "My Margaret can handle most anything."

Mother beamed.

Mother takes the wheel. Photo by Wilbur Curtis for the Memphis Press-Scimitar, 1957

As the weeks passed, and after our Ford station wagon had been retrofitted, Mother's confidence and skill increased to the point that she was able to drive in traffic like a pro. She learned to respond immediately and calmly to the unexpected, like jaywalkers who step off the curb against the light.

And she did so without so much as a dent or a scratch or a smudge on the whitewall tires. When she passed her driver's test and got her driver's license, she felt like the world had finally opened for her. She cried tears of relief, tears of joy. Dad celebrated by taking her out to dinner at a fancy restaurant and toasting her with champagne.

By now we'd moved to a slightly larger house in La Puente, about an hour east of the UCLA campus so Dad wouldn't have such a long commute to and from work. Being able to drive made it much easier for Mother to acclimate to her new environment. Everyone drove in LA, and now she could as well. Running to the market for a few things for dinner was a breeze.

Bob and I were excited about it too. She could drive us to school and pick us up. She could take us to ball games and school events and downtown to go shopping. Maybe she would even take us to Disneyland!

As news of Mother's achievement spread, she started to receive invitations to speak at church gatherings and civic groups. She dazzled an unnamed reporter for the *San Gabriel Valley Daily Tribune* whose feature, entitled "Loss of both arms fails to halt La Puente housewife," was published in July.

Mother in her kitchen. Photo by Wilbur Curtis

Margaret Chanin "is a source of wonder and inspiration to many in the La Puente community," the feature began. "A major pitfall in overcoming a handicap, she indicates, is the danger of 'using it as a crutch' to excuse failure to adjust to life. She agrees with the theory that a well-adjusted person is only 'slowed down momentarily' by disaster and 'comes out pretty well after a normal period of despondency and discouragement.'"

Mother acknowledged that Dad had been there all along, to encourage her and urge her to strive even beyond the limits of her capability. As the reporter put it, "she implies that by far her greatest triumph was her marriage to Dr. Chanin 'for love and not security.'"

"In her determined quest to become self-reliant and 'lead a normal life,' Mrs. Chanin has achieved mastery of a secondary gift – impressing strangers and acquaintances with an illusion that her handicaps are not important. And, miraculously, the illusion becomes a fact, even to Mrs. Chanin, as she perceives in her own life that a pattern has evolved that makes her more useful as a member of society, perhaps, than if she had escaped tragedy."

Progress on the left stump was not going as well. In fact, it was exceedingly painful. In September 1955, Mother underwent a second revision to try to relieve the pain and find out what was going on. After removing the scar, her surgeons found the end of the stump covered with a mass of inflammatory connective tissue. Part of the bone graft had died. In medical terms, it was necrotic. The obviously necrotic tissue was removed, and the length of the graft was reduced by a little more than a third of an inch to about three inches. The wound was closed loosely with black suture and allowed to drain. Eventually, the stump healed and became, as the surgeons described it, "perfectly padded with soft parts that were freely moveable and non-painful."

After about six months, in April 1956, Mother tried the left-arm prosthesis again. "Approximately three-and-a-half years after the graft was implanted, she demonstrated painless function of an arm stump that had previously been useless … Her right stump was, of course, more efficient, and she wore her left prosthesis only when she was not wearing the right prosthesis."

Earlier, she had attempted a shoulder harness for bilateral fitting, but the harness so restricted her movement that she found she could not use both prostheses at the same time. She tried to use the left arm to anchor a roaster pan while she cleaned it with a scrub brush held in the double hook at the end of her right arm, but the harness was so tight she couldn't maneuver the pan in the sink without becoming exhausted. Realizing the men who had worked on her prosthesis might be skeptical, she took the roaster pan with her the next time she met with them.

"Look, y'all," she told them. "Watch what happens. Why have a second arm if you can't do anything with it?"

When she finished her demonstration, one of the engineers said, "Well, Margaret, you've convinced us. If somebody has got an amputation as high as yours, we should strive for one good arm and not worry about the second one."

In an article for a medical journal published in 1959, Marshall Urist and Robert Mazet concluded that their daring bone-graft procedure to lengthen an upper-arm stump so that it was more functional was of limited value. But while their experiment had ultimately failed, the operation on her right stump and the subsequent fitting of her first lightweight, comfortable, and truly functional prosthesis had truly transformed Mother's life. And while the left prosthesis was by no means as functional as the right, she could still use it from time to time, when the skin of the right stump became irritated from overuse.

In the spring of 1956, as Mother was completing the training program and her course of surgery, a story about her was published in *Coronet*, a pocket-sized, general interest magazine like *Reader's Digest*, with a reported circulation of 2.7 million readers. The five-page, 1,500-word spread, entitled "Mother of Courage," was written by Joseph Stocker, and featured photos of Mother behind the wheel of our station wagon, baking cupcakes, helping 5-year-old Robert get into his jacket, and spending family time with us playing Chinese Checkers on the living room rug.

Joseph Stocker was particularly suited to chronicle Mother's life. A former reporter for the *Oklahoma City Times*, he served in the 45th Infantry Division, which during World War II saw action in Italy, France, and Germany, and which helped liberate the Dachau concentration camp northwest of Munich. He wrote for the *45th Division News* and for a time worked with the celebrated cartoonist Bill Mauldin. After the war, Stocker took up freelance writing and moved to Phoenix, where he helped desegregate the public schools and exposed the "Gentleman's Agreement" that had quietly excluded Jews from many of the city's hotels and resorts. He died in 2003 at the age of 90.

In introducing the feature about Mother, the editors of *Coronet* asked, "What is courage?" In her case, they wrote, it is "a dogged, day-in, day-out bravery so overwhelming that you can only marvel."

Brave? Certainly. But when we were young, Bob and I didn't appreciate how extraordinary she was. To us, she was simply Mother. In the handmade Mother's Day card I gave to her in 1956, when I was 7, I printed the following message in crayon on folded construction paper:

Thank you for the picnic lunches out in the backyard, Mother.
Thank you for letting me go over to my friends' house.
I love you best of all.
Philip

By now we had moved again, this time to 1426 S. 4th Avenue in Arcadia, just three and a half miles west of the City of Hope National Medical Center in the foothills of the San Gabriel Mountains. Three moves in three years. We were all discovering Dad's wanderlust. But at least part of the reason was air pollution. The air quality in the San Gabriel Valley was rapidly declining—the result of California's love affair with the automobile and dust plumes sent up by a nearby rock quarry. I suffered most from the smog. So did Dad. Whenever we traveled on the freeway, our eyes would burn, even with the car windows rolled up. Unfortunately, the move to Arcadia didn't solve the problem. The air quality was just as bad.

It wasn't just the dirty air. The cost of living in Los Angeles was high, and Mother felt she'd gone about as far as she could in the UCLA program. She longed to be closer to her parents. So, in the fall of 1956, Dad piled us into the station wagon after the sun had set to begin our long journey back east. He wanted to cross California's Mojave Desert at night so we could avoid its brutal daytime temperatures. Several days later, we arrived at Haskins' and Mae's farm in Arkansas. Dad accepted a one-year position teaching chemistry at Memphis State University, filling in for a chemistry professor who was on sabbatical. As the fall term began, we moved into a house at 1736 S. Perkins Road, just east of the Memphis city line.

Shortly after our arrival, Mother took another driving test to get a Tennessee license. Dad drove her to the Tennessee Highway Patrol's driver license station. Mother whipped through the written exam, completing the answers with a pencil held between her teeth and turning the pages with her prosthesis. The state trooper who administered the test was dubious. His incredulity increased when Mother got behind the wheel of her specially equipped Ford station wagon. Swallowing his skepticism, he climbed into the passenger seat next to her and off they drove. Catherine Meacham, a reporter for the *Memphis Press-Scimitar*, picked up the story from there.

"When they returned to the station," she wrote, "the trooper took off his hat. 'Lady,' he said, 'mind if I tell you something? You're the best driver I ever saw.'"

Chapter Ten
Dark Father

In Memphis, Mother was active in the PTA, serving as its representative to the City Council and chairing its Parent Education Committee. Bob and I attended the Memphis Training School, an elementary school on the Memphis State campus that trained student teachers. Bob and I were captivated—we'd never had such enthusiastic and attractive young women instructors!

On weekends, we were at our grandparents' 80-acre farm near Osceola, Arkansas, and during the summer, we practically lived there.

"My memories of the farm are wonderful," Bob would recall years later. In the morning, we'd rise early to help Granddad milk the cows. "Then he would go into the kitchen and make a huge breakfast with homemade biscuits, gravy, grits, eggs, sausage, bacon, cow brains, and jelly and preserves made from his fruit trees," Bob wrote.

At harvest time, Granddad encouraged us to climb up in the pecan trees that surrounded the farmhouse and shake the limbs to dislodge the mature pecans. We'd scoop up thousands of the scattered nuts from the ground and bag them. Granddad sold them at the local farmer's market. He'd take us dove hunting and drive us across the Mississippi River to Reelfoot Lake on the Tennessee/Kentucky border. When the fishing was good, we'd come home with a dozen or more bluegill, catfish, or largemouth bass, and Grandmother and Mother would cook them up in a skillet for dinner.

Granddad was a quiet, kind man. "He was always doing for others," Bob observed. "He loved everyone, and everyone loved him ... We would drive around to the widow ladies' homes, giving away eggs and tomatoes."

Bob compared him to Grandpa Walton, the wise and warm character played by the actor Will Geer in the 1970s television show, *The Waltons*. "I can still smell his cigars and the inside of his old Ford pickup," Bob wrote. "To me, he seemed like the best and strongest man in the world. He taught us to hunt and fish, but most important, he showed me how a man can laugh at himself and his mistakes and be respected."

In my brother's eyes, Dad suffered by comparison.

Haskins and his grandsons, Robert and Philip

"My father never met anyone that he couldn't find fault with," Bob wrote. "Nothing seemed to restrain my father from criticizing those in whom he found fault. Most people hesitate to voice all of their critical thoughts, because they want to survive in the job market and maintain relationships with friends and family. Not my father. If he saw something that was wrong or that he didn't like, he was quick to mention it. No one was safe from his scrutiny."

After leaving Los Angeles, Dad seemed to lose focus. He resented the time we spent with our grandparents. He thought they were spoiling us, and he and Mother quarreled about that. Gradually, he began to avoid our weekend trips to the farm. "This may have been the beginning of the end for him," Bob concluded.

Dad taught chemistry at Memphis State for a year but when, in the fall of 1957, he refused to give passing grades to members of the football team, who had failed his course, so they wouldn't lose their eligibility to play college ball, his contract was terminated, just as it had been in Evansville.

He took the first job he could find—as a chemist at Humko, a leading manufacturer of high-grade shortening that later was absorbed by Kraft Foods. Dad would bring home mouth-watering pies and cakes that had been freshly baked in the company's test kitchen.

Bob and I admired our father for standing up for what was right, even if it meant losing his job. But, as Bob put it, "Being smarter than everyone else can be a real handicap ... Although I respect him for his convictions, I suspect this was another symptom of his depression, unhappiness, and inability to coexist with other human beings. He wanted everyone to conform to his perfect standard and had no patience with other peoples' flaws. I admire him for his high standards of behavior and morals, but we live in an imperfect world, inhabited by imperfect people."

Two years later, Dad found a job in Clemson, South Carolina, teaching textile chemistry in the School of Textiles at the Clemson Agricultural and Mechanical College, now Clemson University. We were on the move once again.

It was during this period that Bob and I developed our special bond. Since we moved so often, leaving friends behind, my brother became my constant companion and my combatant. We played together and wrestled for hours, never to hurt the other but to establish who was stronger. As I had a two-year-and-eight-day head start, I had an advantage. Still, Bob was persistent. As many times as I threw him off the bed, he'd come right back for another round.

The move to Clemson was hard on Bob, who was 9 years old at the time. His fourth-grade teacher was a harsh, critical woman. "I could not please her," he recalled years later. "Other than my father, I had never met anyone like her, and I refused to put up with it. I spent a great deal of time in the hall outside her door and my mother would let me stay home from school whenever I wanted. She would go to the library and bring me home a stack of books. That year, I discovered reading as a means of escaping the painful reality of fourth grade. We also had a TV and I learned to escape by watching and dreaming of another reality more pleasant than the one I was trapped in."

Bob wasn't only talking about school. As we grew older, Dad became increasingly irritable with us, liable to blow up at the least provocation.

Our father had many good qualities. He valued education and the life of the mind. He stimulated my interest in learning, helped me with my homework, and took pride in our academic achievements. I clearly remember our move from California. I was 8, and Bob was 6. As Dad drove across the Mojave Desert at night, he quizzed us in math. "If apples cost 8 cents," he asked, "how many apples can you buy for 32 cents?" Then came the trick question: "If you have three apples, four oranges, and two bananas, what do you do?" Of course, we knew the answer because Dad valued being funny above almost everything else. "Make fruit salad!"

Then there was the father I did not have, the man that poet Robert Bly might call the Dark Father. My Dark Father was a man of anger and impatience, a perfectionist with a strong need to be in control. In truth, Dad probably should not have had children, because he always needed children to be Little Adults. Mother recognized this. "He was a good father to the children when they were little," she told an interviewer years later. "They never had a conflict with him until they had a mind of their own and a will of their own … Then he became very strict with them."

There were myriad rules that my brother and I had to obey. As a boy, I fantasized that our father must have kept a notebook where he wrote down 200 rules for how his children should behave, and in another corresponding column, the punishment for each infraction. For much of my childhood, it seemed, I was either confined to the house for a week or to the yard for a month as punishment for one rule or another I'd broken.

This was also the late 1950s, early 1960s, when corporal punishment was widely accepted. Quite often when we needed to be "corrected," Dad would pull out his belt or a leather strap and give us a few whacks on our backsides. As I grew older, I was able to escape his beatings by outrunning him. When I was 10 or 11, however, he insisted that my behavior was so bad I should be sent away to "a school in Bell Buckle." The Webb School in Bell Buckle, Tennessee, is one of the most highly regarded college preparatory schools in the country. But to my young ears, the name of the town conjured up images of even worse punishments. Mother's only recourse was to break into tears to get my father to back off.

Bob believed our paternal grandfather, the wholesale produce dealer after whom I was named, was responsible for Dad becoming a sour-faced "critical perfectionist with almost no social skills."

Born in 1896 in Newark, New Jersey, the son of Ukrainian immigrants, Grandfather Philip was not interested in Dad's intellectual pursuits or academic achievements. Rigidly opinionated and judgmental, he wanted his son to open a drug store instead of going to college. Meanwhile, Grandmother Minnie doted on her firstborn child, lavishing more attention on him than she did her husband. This no doubt was another source of considerable friction in the Chanin household. Recalled Deenie Wright, the daughter of Dad's younger sister (and only sibling) Carol, "the fighting that went on in that house was a horror."

Dad had started out in his marriage to Mother so open and generous. But with every perceived slight and disappointment, he became less the eager romantic who'd won her heart 14 years before, and more a caustic replica of his own father.

Childrearing was a source of frequent conflict between my parents. On a few occasions, when Dad felt Mother was being too lenient, he'd storm out of the house and not return until the following day. Increasingly, Mother found herself caught between Dad's unhappiness and our welfare.

"My mom was forced to walk a tightrope of discretion because of her dependence on him," Bob noted in a recollection of his childhood that he wrote years later. "She saw the damage he was doing to their sons and himself but was careful when trying to balance his criticism with reality. She knew that if a conflict occurred between them, she would very soon afterwards be asking him to bathe or dress or feed her … I think my father also realized how dependent he was on her for emotional stability and rewarding social relationships."

This was only one side of the story, of course. For Mother was a woman of faith. Whenever Dad pulled up stakes and moved us again, she found a new church home. Not only that, but she witnessed. Whether she found herself in big-city LA or small-town Clemson, Mother would give inspirational talks to church and community and women's groups about the challenges she had met and surmounted—thanks in large part to her determination, her family's unwavering love and support, and her abiding faith. It was not surprising that others in her orbit were bathed more in light than in darkness. One of them was the Rev. Charles Anthony Arrington, pastor of our new faith family at First Baptist Church of Clemson.

On February 23, 1960, Arrington devoted half of the church's four-page bulletin, *The Tie*, to telling Mother's story, and Dad's.

"The relation of Margaret and Martin is a beautiful one," he wrote. "She frankly says that he has done more to help her adjust than anyone or anything else, and that if he were a different kind of person they simply could not get along as a family. He is Jewish in background, and she an ardent Baptist, yet this difference is no barrier to them at all. He encourages her in all her religious work and is as regular in attendance at our church services as any member we have."

Whether she speaks at church retreats at nearby Ridgecrest in North Carolina, or 1,500 miles away at the Glorieta Baptist Assembly in New Mexico, "he is right there with her," Arrington continued. "Margaret's loss of arms is a joint affair with them, and they both accept it together."

Learning to drive a car, as she did in Los Angeles, seemed an impossible task. "But to a woman of courage with a husband to stand by her, little is impossible," he concluded. "She has long since stopped thinking about herself as handicapped ... Perhaps birds think of human beings as handicapped because they do not have wings, but we do not seem to think so. We get along. And so does Margaret Chanin."

Arrington's depiction of Dad as devoted was not far off the mark. As difficult and as troubled as he was, our father never stopped trying to help my mother and improve the lives of others through his wildly ingenious inventions. While in Clemson, he incorporated the Chanin Products Company, through which he registered a breast pump that would enable women to express and refrigerate breast milk for their infants, and a "desensitizer," a complicated mechanism for applying a desensitizing solution to a tooth prior to beginning dental work.

Most useful to Mother was the compact "food elevator" on wheels Dad invented in 1962 that mechanically raised and lowered a sturdy platform along a metal pole. This enabled her to transfer awkward and heavy containers, like a pitcher full of milk or a cast-iron skillet, from the refrigerator or stove to the kitchen counter without having to grasp and balance them with the hook of her prosthetic arm. Like the modifications to the car that enabled Mother to drive, his food elevator gave her a measure of freedom, control, and accomplishment she could not have attained on her own.

I don't know how well Mother and Arrington knew each other. But I believe he helped prepare her for the next chapter of her life. For Charles Anthony Arrington was a remarkable man. Dark haired, with a firm mouth and penetrating gaze, he was in his own way as determined a rule-breaker as was Mother.

Born in rural Greenwood County, South Carolina, in 1912, Arrington had set out to become an engineer. He got his bachelor's degree in civil engineering from Clemson A & M in 1933. But he found his true calling as a minister, earning master's degrees in theology from Southern Seminary in Louisville, Kentucky, and Union Seminary in New York City. During World War II, he was a chaplain with the Army's Sixth Armored Division. After storming Utah Beach in Normandy in 1944, the "Super Sixth," as it was called, was assigned to General George S. Patton's Third Army. The division fought its way across France and took part in the Battle of the Bulge, the largest and bloodiest battle fought by the United States in the war.

Moving quickly into central Germany as Hitler's army retreated, Arrington and his fellow soldiers spent the next few months freeing Allied POWs. On April 11, 1945, they entered the notorious Buchenwald concentration camp in east-central Germany. More than 56,000 inmates—Jews, Poles and other Slavs, political prisoners, the mentally ill and physically disabled—died there during the war and were buried in mass graves. The camp's SS guards, Hitler's elite troops, fled days before the Allies arrived, yet some 21,000 inmates remained, many of them skeletal and too weakened from starvation to escape on their own. What Arrington witnessed at Buchenwald changed the course of his life. After retiring from the pulpit in 1971, he and his wife Ottie spent six years as associate missionaries for the Southern Baptist Foreign Mission Board, serving English language churches in Lebanon, Greece, and Spain, and working with Christian groups in Saudi Arabia.

Arrington died in 1980. But perhaps the most profound impact he made during his life was during his years in Clemson. The civil rights movement was already rumbling when he arrived at First Baptist Church in 1956. Despite the growing clamor for integration, many of the churches of South Carolina, reflecting the dominant social structure of the time, remained stubbornly segregated. Church leaders accused civil rights activists of being communists. Integration, they alleged, would lead to "mongrelization of the races." They quoted scripture to justify their position.

First Baptist Church was different. Formerly known as the Clemson College Baptist Church, its congregation consisted largely of college students and faculty members and their families. It held ecumenical services and welcomed worshippers of different faiths. Beginning in the early 1950s the church reached out to different races as well. Arrington took up the torch of integration.

During a Race Relations Conference held by the South Carolina Baptist Convention in 1964 he declared, "When some future history is written it will doubtless be recorded that in these times of racial tension, the Christian churches did comparatively little to promote understanding and goodwill. We White Baptists pride ourselves on being a great missionary people, and yet we have done almost nothing to help the Negro brethren in our midst."

Five years later he launched "Race Relations Sunday," a service that encouraged all races to discuss and work together. As former Clemson graduate student and now Greenville minister Lawson Clary put it in his 2006 master's thesis, "A Church on the Move," Arrington transformed First Baptist Church of Clemson into a "cutting-edge religious body on both social and spiritual fronts."

Charles Anthony Arrington was not the first remarkable person in Mother's life—nor would he be the last. In 1941, Dr. Frederick C. Elliott, dean of the Texas Dental College, stood beside Mother's hospital bed and told her she would return to school. Two years later, her speech teacher at Baylor, Sara Lowrey, inspired her to believe in the impossible. At the University of Michigan, Dr. Kenneth A. Easlick helped her imagine a career in public health dentistry. Dr. Eugene Murphy was her connection to the prosthetics training program in Los Angeles. And had it not been for Dr. Charles O. Bechtol, who in 1954 selected Mother for the experimental surgery program at UCLA, she probably would never have learned to drive a car.

I know Mother believed that God had a hand in these seemingly chance encounters with remarkable men and women. For her, such a meeting was like an open door. She never hesitated. She was curious—and fearless. She always walked through the door into the unknown. She always took advantage of a new opportunity. And because of her pluck and faith, Mother was able to change her life, and the lives of those around her, for the better.

My parents had intended to buy a lot in Clemson and put down roots, but three years after we arrived, in 1962, Dad was notified, once again, that his teaching contract at the college would not be renewed. A friend or a relative of one of the big donors to the School of Textiles wanted his job, so Dad had to go. Our next stop was Florence, Alabama, where Dad found work as Chair of the Science Department at Florence State College, now the University of North Alabama.

Situated on the shores of the Tennessee River, the cluster of small towns known as Florence, Sheffield, Tuscumbia, and Muscle Shoals in the early 1960s comprised a melting pot of industrial, intellectual, and musical might. Sheffield was the site of the first aluminum smelting facility built by the Reynolds Metal Company to provide lightweight materials for the burgeoning aircraft industry. Next-door Tuscumbia was the hometown of the renowned disability rights activist Helen Keller, while Muscle Shoals' FAME Studios were creating a new soulful sound in popular music.

Across the river was Florence, home of the oldest college in Alabama. Formerly a state teachers' college, by the late 1940s Florence State had expanded its offerings to meet the postwar demand for engineers and scientists. Tiny Florence, Alabama, was feeding the technological revolution that was transforming America, and Dad wanted to be a part of it. He wasn't the only one. Across the street from our new home, on the corner of Winston Street and Tune Avenue, lived a physical chemist who worked for Reynolds, his wife, a microbiologist, and their two small children.

Our families bonded almost immediately. Like Mother and Dad, Nolan, and Helen Richards, who were originally from New Zealand, valued education. They believed, said their physician son, Dr. Bruce Richards, that "if you pushed the boundaries of your curiosity to wherever it led you, good things would happen."

At first Mother was the neighborhood novelty, the "lady with no arms."

But soon 6-year-old Bruce and his younger sister Robin were frequent visitors. "I remember their hardwood floors," Bruce recalls, "because my sister and I would skate on our socked feet, and once she fell down and got a big splinter in her butt and had to go to the hospital."

Bruce marveled at how Dad had "engineered the house" for Mother. He'd installed a special oven she could open with her prosthesis, and special drawer handles so she could open drawers with her toe. "She had incredibly long legs and a high kick," Bruce said. "She had a prehensile great toe, and she could do things that you and I would do with our hands."

While she was a "full-time mom," as Bruce put it, Mother took time to listen to the neighbors' children. She talked with them on their level and gave them books to read like *Black Beauty* and *Bob, Son of Battle*, about a sheepdog. One evening, while she was taking a walk around the block with Bruce in the cool of the evening, he told her that, like his parents, he was mad about sailing. Afterwards she bought him a copy of *Stuart Little*, which features a mouse winning a sailboat race.

Mother also passed onto Bruce a pond yacht that had been the prized possession of another little boy in Evanston, Illinois, 30 years earlier. A sailboat had been the cause of her disfigurement. This model could have brought up dark memories of loss and regret. Yet she was able to see it through the eyes of a child, imagining the possibility of victory rather than a more sober "adult" acceptance of limitation and defeat. She understood that parents—and life—are often full of rules that are impossible for children to meet. She wanted the children, and all the people in her life, to know that they mattered.

Meanwhile, my father had become quite a character on the Florence campus, just as he had years before in Evansville when he won the "Ugly Man" contest. Known for his proclivity for telling jokes, he could frequently be spotted wearing a distinctive red cap topped with a rabbit's tail. "Learn to laugh at yourself," Dad told a reporter for the student newspaper in February 1963, perhaps taking a lesson out of Mother's book. "'Laugh and the whole world laughs with you; weep and you weep alone.'"

Yet Dad had once again become a thorn in the side of college officials. This time it was because he reported poor workmanship in the new science building that had just opened. Dad's complaints about laboratory vents that didn't work properly and steam lines that had been installed incorrectly didn't fall on deaf ears, but they weren't appreciated either. That spring he was informed, once again, that his contract for the 1963-1964 school year would not be renewed. But just as he had several times before, Dad bounced back. He applied for—and was granted—a post-doctoral fellowship in the pharmacology department at Vanderbilt University in Nashville, Tennessee. In June 1963, we were on the road once again.

Seven-year-old Bruce was devastated. But he and Mother would meet again.

Chapter Eleven
A Special Burden

Upon our arrival in Nashville in the summer of 1963, we rented the bottom floor of a two-story bungalow at 3822 Richland Avenue for $100 a month. Located just off West End Avenue, the house was within walking distance of West End High School, where I would begin 10th grade. Bob, who'd just turned 13, was two grades behind me. It didn't take long for Mother to find a place of worship at nearby Immanuel Baptist Church on Belle Meade Boulevard.

Conceived in 1905 by a group of investors led by Guilford Dudley Sr., co-founder of the Nashville-based Life & Casualty Insurance Company, the Richland-West End neighborhood was one of the city's first planned subdivisions. Most of the homes were built for doctors, lawyers, businessmen, and other members of the upper-middle class, but by the 1950s, the neighborhood had shifted largely to families headed by blue-collar workers and college students. One of the most prominent early residents, Morris Frank, established the nation's first guide dog training school in Nashville in 1929. Years later, Richland Avenue would figure in a Disney movie about Frank's life entitled *Love Leads the Way*.

Down the block from us, at 3806 Richland, lived George and Betty Weitemeyer and their five children. George was a printer who worked for

Rand McNally's ticket-printing division in Nashville. As Bob and I went to school with their children, it didn't take us long to become, well, neighborly.

"As a young boy in the 60s, I did notice her car," the youngest Weitemeyer boy, Keith told me. "I recall a full-size Pontiac with a marble ring affixed to the steering wheel, and a hook device on the gearshift for her to operate the car. She was an enthusiastic driver ... not at all hesitant in her driving. The most unusual thing back then might have been that she worked all day every day outside the home. She dressed for success and wore perfume. She was a professional, put-together woman who could make an impression just by walking into the room."

It is true. When she was going out, Mother always dressed impeccably, including her jewelry and perfume. With her new prosthesis, she even could apply her makeup. She always endeavored to put her best foot forward.

That's what women did in 1963, especially in southern cities like Nashville. On Saturdays, women still wore their best dresses, high heels, and hats to go shopping downtown at the department stores that lined Church Street—Harveys, Cain-Sloan and Castner Knott. Harveys, which covered an entire block of Church Street, from 6th Avenue to 5th, was not just a store—it was a destination. Harveys had the first escalators in Middle Tennessee. The main floor had a circus-like atmosphere, with several carousel horses salvaged from a defunct amusement park and live monkeys in a cage. One could spend a day there, shopping and eating at its lunch counter—a long row of short-backed stools that swiveled on metal poles and which faced the grill. Among the most popular orders at Harveys was its famous apple pie.

Every Christmas beginning in 1953 and until 1967, store owner Fred Harvey, and later his son Fred Jr., installed a Nativity scene in front of Nashville's full-size concrete replica of the ancient Greek Parthenon in Centennial Park, across West End Avenue from Vanderbilt University. Thousands of people strolled by the panorama, illuminated at night by colored lights and giant flood lamps, to view plaster statues of palm trees and angels, Wise Men on their camels, shepherds and their sheep, Mary and Joseph, and the Baby Jesus in the manger.

Especially during the hot, carefree days of summer, the children of

Nashville would clamor to go to Cascade Plunge and Fair Park at the Tennessee State Fairgrounds. Opened in 1923, the Cascade Plunge was Nashville's largest swimming pool. It had two giant water slides and a 60-foot-tall diving platform. Across the way was Fair Park, an unending source of surprise and amusement for adults and children alike. There was the Deep Dip, a rickety-looking wooden roller coaster that opened in 1924 and which would be replaced in 1965 by the more formidable Skyliner. The park also featured a 55-foot Ferris wheel, Tilt-a-Whirl, bumper cars, a train pulling boxcars for children to ride, a miniature golf course, and even an organ grinder with a live capuchin monkey that took money from delighted customers.

Nashville in 1963 claimed slightly more than 170,000 residents. Another 230,000 lived within the confines of Davidson County. That year, the separate city and county governments merged. A metropolitan government made sense economically as it increased the tax base and enabled an expansion of government services throughout the county. And yet Nashville was still a largely segregated city. Thanks to the efforts of thousands of citizens emboldened by the civil rights movement, the lunch counters in the city's downtown department stores had opened to Black shoppers as well as whites in 1960. Under federal edict, the restrooms and waiting areas in bus and train stations in Nashville and throughout the South no longer were separated by race. Progress in other areas stalled, however, in 1961, when student activists called for the desegregation of Nashville's public swimming pools. The Nashville Parks and Recreation Board responded by closing the pools—including Cascade Plunge—to everyone.

In Davidson County, as had been the case in Flint, Michigan, the postwar shift to the suburbs only seemed to entrench racial segregation and its debilitating effects. Local housing and school construction policies favored the predominantly white, middle-class residents of the new suburban neighborhoods over downtown, where most of the city's lower-income Black children and their families lived. Inner-city schools were neglected, overcrowded, and in poor condition. Desegregation of the lower grades had begun in 1957, but comprehensive desegregation of Nashville's public schools would not be achieved until 1971, when a federal court order required busing to achieve racial balance.

This was the Nashville we moved to in 1963, a city that was being remolded and transformed by the momentum of social change.

The transformation had begun nearly a decade earlier, when the United States Supreme Court ruled unanimously in *Brown v. Board of Education* that legally sanctioned racial segregation of public schools was in violation of the Equal Protection Clause of the U.S. Constitution. The following year, in 1955, attorneys representing the Nashville chapter of the National Association for the Advancement of Colored People (NAACP) filed suit to end the segregation of the Nashville's public schools. They were Z. Alexander Looby, the chief NAACP attorney in Tennessee and one of two Black members of the Nashville City Council; Looby's young associate, Avon Williams Jr., who would later become the first Black elected to the Tennessee State Senate; and Williams' first cousin, Thurgood Marshall, chief counsel for the NAACP Legal Defense and Education Fund in New York who, in 1967, became the first Black justice appointed to the U.S. Supreme Court.

The Nashville Board of Education responded to the lawsuit with a plan to desegregate one grade per year, beginning with first grade, in the fall of 1957. Although angrily opposed by pro-segregation demonstrators, the plan proceeded. On September 9, 1957, 15 Black first-graders were admitted to six previously all-white elementary schools. The next day, a dynamite explosion destroyed a wing of Hattie Cotton Elementary School in East Nashville where one of the Black children had enrolled. No one was hurt, and the bombing was roundly condemned. Eleven of the children returned to their newly integrated classrooms without further incident.

Two years later, in the fall of 1959, the Rev. James Lawson, an ordained Methodist minister and one of three Black students at Vanderbilt University Divinity School, began teaching workshops on nonviolent principles and techniques at Clark Memorial United Methodist Church in predominantly Black North Nashville. Sponsored by a local civil rights organization, the Nashville Christian Leadership Council, and by the Southern Christian Leadership Conference, which was led by the Rev. Martin Luther King Jr., the workshops were attended by students from Nashville's four traditionally Black colleges—Fisk University, Meharry Medical College, the Tennessee Agricultural & Industrial

State College (today's Tennessee State University), and the American Baptist Theological Seminary (now American Baptist College).

Among those Lawson trained were Marion Barry, who years later served two terms as mayor of the District of Columbia, and John Lewis, who would go on to become a prominent civil rights leader and member of Congress. In late 1959, these students and others began a campaign to desegregate the lunch counters at Nashville's downtown department stores. At the time, Black customers were welcome to shop at Woolworths and other stores, but they would not be served at the lunch counters.

The Nashville Christian Leadership Council initially attempted to negotiate with the department stores, but when the stores did not respond, the demonstrations began. The students would sit on the stools at the lunch counters without saying a word and, when they were refused service, they would just as calmly and silently get up and leave.

While the first few demonstrations took place without incident, trouble arrived on Saturday, February 27, 1960. As the students sat at the lunch counter at McClellan's department store on Fifth Avenue North, a crowd of white hecklers surrounded them, calling them names and blowing cigarette smoke in their faces. One of the white students participating in the sit-in was pulled off his stool and beaten. He did not resist, and his fellow protestors sat in silence while he was punched and kicked, adhering to the practice of nonviolent resistance in which they had been so carefully schooled. Police waited to enter the store until the attack was over, and then they arrested the beaten student.

Down the street at Woolworth's, the protestors were burnt with lit cigarettes and spit upon. White men marched up to the second floor of the lunch counter, where they beat up several protestors and pushed others down the stairs. The injured were taken to segregated hospitals for treatment. Dozens of students were arrested and taken to jail while an unruly white crowd cheered from the street outside.

On March 3, Lawson was expelled from Vanderbilt for allegedly inciting demonstrators to "break the law," even though there was no ordinance in Nashville that expressly prohibited integrated lunch counters. After most of the divinity school faculty submitted their resignations and more than 100 others signed a petition supporting Lawson, university officials offered a compromise agreement that would have allowed him to complete his degree. But by then, he had decided to transfer to Boston University.

As the sit-ins continued, the protestors were met with more jeers and abuse. Then, at about 5:30 a.m. on Tuesday, April 19, 1960, a dynamite bomb was tossed from a passing car through the front window of the North Nashville home of Z. Alexander Looby, the students' lead attorney. Although the front of the house was destroyed, Looby and his wife, who were sleeping in a back room, were uninjured. The blast was so powerful, however, that it blew out windows in nearby Meharry Medical College and Hubbard Hospital, injuring several students.

Later that day, students from Tennessee A&I began marching toward Jefferson Street and 18th Avenue North, where they met up with others from Fisk University and Pearl High School. By the time they reached downtown, an estimated 2,000 students, both Black and white, had joined the march. They walked in complete silence, three abreast, until they reached the City Hall Plaza, where Mayor Ben West was waiting for them outside. When asked by Diane Nash, one of the leaders of the movement, if he felt it was wrong to discriminate against people because of their race, the mayor admitted that he did.

The next evening the Rev. Martin Luther King Jr. addressed a capacity crowd in the Fisk University auditorium. He praised the students for modeling non-violent resistance and sent a message to those who opposed them. "We will meet the capacity to inflict suffering with the capacity to endure suffering," King said. "We will say, do what you will to us, but we will wear you down by our capacity to suffer."

Eventually the merchants relented, and on May 10, 1960, Nashville's department store lunch counters were opened to Black customers.

In 1961, students from American Baptist, Fisk, and Tennessee A&I joined the "Freedom Rides" to protest segregated waiting rooms at bus stations throughout the South. On May 20, 1961, a white mob wielding baseball bats and iron pipes set upon them as they pulled into a bus depot in

Montgomery, Alabama. Among those beaten was John Seigenthaler, a representative of the U.S. Justice Department, who was left unconscious in the street. The Freedom Riders were undeterred. Four days later another group that included 14 A&I students arrived in Jackson, Mississippi, where they were promptly arrested and taken to jail. The A&I students were summarily expelled for their actions. A federal court later overturned the expulsions, and in September the Interstate Commerce Commission ordered the bus stations to desegregate. Seigenthaler went on to become editor and publisher of Nashville's morning paper, *The Tennessean*.

Shortly before our arrival in Nashville, on May 18, 1963, President John F. Kennedy was the featured speaker at Vanderbilt University's 90th anniversary convocation. "This nation is now engaged in a continuing debate about the rights of a portion of its citizens," he observed. "The determination to secure these rights is in the highest traditions of American freedom. In these moments of tragic disorder, a special burden rests on the educated men and women of our country to reject the temptations of prejudice and violence and to reaffirm the values of freedom and law on which our free society depends."

Six months later, Kennedy was assassinated in Dallas, Texas.

We had moved to Nashville during a time of great upheaval. Soon Mother and Dad would be swept into the maelstrom of progress and resistance that was engulfing the city. Yet they also would contribute to the turn of events, each in their own way. They would answer, and help fulfill, a young president's call for freedom and justice for all.

Chapter Twelve
The Salt Wagon Story

Dad had hoped that his job at Vanderbilt would lead to an offer to join the faculty. That was not to be. In 1964, after several months of looking, he secured a position teaching organic chemistry at predominantly Black Tennessee A&I, known familiarly as Tennessee State University. The *Pittsburgh (Pennsylvania) Courier*, one of the leading Black newspapers in the country, celebrated Dad's arrival by publishing a large photo of him and five other faculty members with doctoral degrees in its October 24 edition. "Six more doctorate degrees," the caption read, bring to 60 the total number of full-time "terminal degree holders" on the faculty. This was a significant achievement for a university that had been established in 1912 as the Tennessee Agricultural and Industrial Normal School for Negroes.

TSU was located at the western end of Jefferson Street, the heart of Nashville's thriving Black community. Twenty blocks east, at the corner of 18th Avenue, were two other prominent, predominantly Black institutions of higher learning—Fisk University and Meharry Medical College. Named for the nation's third president, Jefferson Street was lined with businesses, churches and, until the late 1960s, bustling nightclubs. Lower Broadway had the Grand Ole Opry, but North Nashville had Club Revillot and Club Del Morocco, which helped launch the careers of Little Richard in the late 1950s and Jimi Hendrix in the early '60s.

Years later, Little Richard, whose signature song was "Tutti Frutti," recalled that Club Revillot paid him $100 a week. He hadn't yet sold a single record, but whenever he was scheduled to perform, "I packed the house," he said. "You couldn't get in."

By the mid-1960s, TSU had secured an enviable reputation among the nation's historically Black colleges and universities (HBCUs) for its prowess on the athletic field and in the performing arts. The university's football team, the Tigers, won the Black College National Championship five times between 1946 and 1965. The marching band, known as the Aristocrat of Bands, was the first HBCU band to appear on national television (during a National Football League game in 1955), and the first to perform at a presidential inauguration (Kennedy's in 1961).

But it was the women's track team that really put TSU on the map. Under the direction of famed Coach Ed Temple, the "Tigerbelles" brought home their first gold medal from the 1952 Olympics in Helsinki. Eight years later in Rome, Wilma Rudolph, a 20-year-old sprinter from Clarksville, Tennessee, became the first U.S. woman to win three gold medals in a single Olympics. At the Tokyo Games in October 1964, the Tigerbelles would strike Olympic gold twice more.

Located along a bend in the Cumberland River, TSU was growing by leaps and bounds. Under the leadership of University President Walter S. Davis, enrollment increased from 1,000 to 6,000 students between 1943 and 1965, according to a retrospective published in 2015 by *The Tennessean*. More than 70 percent of TSU's facilities were built during Davis' term. The Arts and Sciences track, the Colleges of Engineering and Education, and the Graduate School were created, and more than 15,000 degrees were awarded.

Mother, meanwhile, immersed herself in home life, in volunteer work as a substitute Sunday School teacher at church, and as a substitute teacher at three of Nashville's still-segregated public high schools, Central, Hillwood, and Overton.

Mother taught everything from boys' gym to sewing. Substitute teachers were scarce, she noted in her 1964 Christmas letter. "You know they are desperate when they call an armless character to teach Sewing and Boys Gym! I do enjoy doing it and I think it helps me to better understand our own teenagers." As busy as she was, having little time, as she put it to "twiddle my thumbs," her schedule as a substitute teacher allowed her to take Bob and me to our ballgames.

I'd started playing organized sports for the first time at the YMCA in Clemson—football, basketball, and baseball. Clemson A & M undergraduates were our coaches, and we played teams in surrounding towns including Spartanburg, Greenville, and Easley. My armless mother would fill up the car with my teammates and drive us to the games. This continued after we moved to Nashville at the start of my 10th-grade year. I was playing basketball and tennis, and running track, and again, until I was old enough to get a driver's license, Mother would drive my teammates and me to our games and events at East High School, Goodlettsville, Franklin, and other high schools around Nashville. Nobody thought anything of it. Mother was just doing what everybody else's mom did in those days, driving the boys to their games.

She also was getting recognition. Each week Emma's Flower and Gift Shop on West End Avenue selected an outstanding community leader for "An Orchid to You" salute, which was broadcast on WSIX, one of Nashville's first FM radio stations. Mother was saluted on August 1, 1965,

Our annual Christmas postcard featured a jovial family portrait.

for her accomplishments as a substitute teacher. During the 1964-1965 school year, she'd worked 125 of the 175 school days. "Her great patience, love of children and trained intelligent mind make her a truly great teacher," the tribute concluded.

A few days later, Mother was setting the rectangular table in the kitchen for dinner when the phone rang. Dad was at the university, and I suppose Bob and I were out with friends as school wouldn't start for another couple of weeks. She walked into the living room, slid the hook of her prosthesis into a ring attachment on the handset of the rotary phone, pulled it free of its cradle and put her ear close to the receiver.

"Hello?"

"Is this Margaret Chanin? Dr. Margaret Chanin?"

"Yes. Who is this?"

"You may not remember me, but we were at school together at Michigan. I'm Eugenia Mobley. Mobley McGinnis now. I'm the chairman of the Department of Preventive Dentistry and Community Health at Meharry Medical College.

"You've heard about Meharry, haven't you? Talk to any Black doctor or dentist in the South, and most of them are graduates of Meharry. But we're not exclusive. White, brown, black – the color of your skin doesn't matter to us. We take the best talent where we can find it, in our student body and in our faculty. That's why I'm calling you."

Mother stammered, but nothing coherent came out of her mouth.

Mobley chuckled. "I've been looking for you for a year," she explained. "I heard you were in Nashville, but I knew you as Margaret Jones. I didn't know how to spell your married name. I only knew it started with a 'C.' Then last week I heard about you on the radio. I'm setting up an oral cancer detection program, and I need an assistant. I would like it very much if you would come work with us."

Over the next several minutes, Mobley described the challenge of oral cancer, especially in the Black community. While the oral cancer death rate for white men had been declining since 1950, it was increasing among Black men at an alarming rate. Tobacco use was a major risk factor. Cancers of the lip, oral cavity, and upper throat are completely treatable if caught early. The problem was that few men received regular dental care.

"We've got to find them," she said, "in the factories, in the nursing homes, even in the prisons – wherever they are."

Mother was trying to listen intently to what Mobley was saying but her heart was pounding so fiercely she feared it would beat right out of her chest.

Years later she recalled, "This was a direct answer to a prayer. For 20 years I had been praying that some way, somehow, I would be in a town that I could use my dental education. And now the prayer had been answered."

"Will you help us?" Mobley's question jarred Mother back to the present.

"It's a wonderful offer," Mother responded, trying to rein in the excitement in her voice. "I will need to talk to my family about this."

"Of course," Mobley responded. "But before you make a final decision, can I at least give you a tour of our facilities? I'd like you to meet some of the faculty, too. How about next week?"

"When I'm not teaching …" Mother said, her voice trailing off.

"Fine. I'll have my administrative assistant call you and we'll set a date. Goodbye, Margaret. Until we meet, then."

Mother managed a weak "thank you and goodbye," and hung up the phone. "I have to sit down," she mumbled to herself. She returned to the kitchen, put the kettle on to boil and brewed a cup of tea. Then she sat at the kitchen table and looked out the window to the grassy backyard. "What about the boys?" she worried.

I was about to begin my senior year at West End High School. Through high school, I was an 'A' student and was always on one team or another—I played basketball and tennis and ran track—but last year, after experiencing stabbing pains in my legs, I was diagnosed with spondylolisthesis, a painful spinal condition caused by the slippage of vertebral discs in the lower back. Not much could be done for it, but physical therapy seemed to help.

And then there was Bob and his frequent headaches. A rising sophomore at West End High, he would turn 15 in about a week. Bob's doctor chalked up his headaches to stress and "growing pains," but Mother worried that something more serious was going on.

Mother's mind drifted back to that horrible day in 1941, and to her mother, standing beside the hospital bed. "The time will come when you will see that there is still a purpose in your life," she was saying. "You will realize that you have a mission."

"I will have to call her," Mother thought. "She will be ecstatic."

Mother didn't say anything to us when we bounded through the back door that afternoon. She waited to share her news until Dad got home from work, and we were seated around the dinner table.

"I got the strangest phone call today," she began, her voice trembling slightly. "I've been offered a job at Meharry Medical College, working with the chairwoman of Preventive Dentistry and Community Health."

"Margaret, that's wonderful!" Dad said excitedly. "Of course, you will accept it, yes? You've been waiting your whole life for this."

Mother glanced over at Bob.

"He'll be fine," Dad said. "He is fine. Aren't you, Robert? How are you feeling? Any headaches today?"

Bob mumbled, his mouth full, and shook his head side to side. Nothing major.

"I agree with Dad," I said. "You should take the job."

A couple of weeks later, Mobley gave Mother a tour of the Meharry campus, a cluster of red-brick buildings across 18th Avenue North from Fisk University, one of the premier predominantly Black liberal arts colleges in the country. Founded in 1876 and chartered in 1915, Meharry was the first medical school for African Americans in the South. It was named for its first financial backer, Samuel Meharry, who with his four brothers helped establish the college with a $15,000 donation.

Meharry, an Irish American landowner and businessman from Tippecanoe County, Indiana, was a strong abolitionist before the Civil War. In the 1820s, the story goes, then-16-year-old Samuel was hauling a load of salt through heavy rain in Kentucky when his wagon slid off the road into a muddy ditch. With nightfall coming, Samuel searched for help. He came across a cabin and a family of recently freed slaves. Although fearful that traders in the area might kidnap them and sell them back into slavery, the family took in the bedraggled and obviously distraught young white man and gave him food and shelter for the night. By morning, the storm had passed and the men in the family helped Samuel free his salt wagon from the mud so he could continue his journey.

"I have no money now," he said as he departed, "but when I am able, I shall do something for your race."

After the Civil War and emancipation, the president of Central Tennessee

College, founded in 1865 by missionaries on behalf of the Methodist Church to provide an opportunity for educational advancement to former slaves, asked Samuel if he would help establish a Medical Department. With his brothers' help, Samuel seized the opportunity to repay a Black family's act of kindness decades before. The first regular year of medical classes began in October 1876. Ten years later, the Dental Department was established, followed by a Pharmacy Department in 1889. By 1896, more than half of the Black physicians practicing in the South were graduates of Meharry Medical College.

"Even today, the majority of Black doctors and dentists in the United States were trained at Meharry and at Howard University in Washington, DC," Mobley said.

By the 1960s, several Meharry graduates who were now members of the faculty had achieved prominence well beyond the campus. Among them were Drs. D.B. Todd, Jr., Nashville's first Black cardiovascular surgeon, and Matthew Walker Sr., chairman of surgery at Meharry who was credited with training more Black surgeons than anyone else in the world.

Walker focused on the needs of poor, underserved and minority communities. In 1947, he launched a rural health initiative in Mound Bayou, an independent Black community in western Mississippi that had been founded in 1887 by former slaves. Under his guidance, Meharry students received part of their training and provided medical and surgical care in the community's Taborian Hospital. Walker also established an inner-city medical clinic on Jefferson Street.

In 1949, he took the bold step of admitting another Meharry graduate, Dr. Dorothy Brown, as a resident in surgery, against the advice of many of his colleagues. At the time, it was widely believed—by male surgeons—that women could not handle the rigors of surgery or surgical training. Brown would prove her skeptics wrong. Under Walker's guidance, she successfully completed five years of surgical residency at Meharry, becoming the first Black woman surgeon in the southern United States.

"That's quite a story," Mother said.

Mobley's story was equally impressive. Born in Birmingham, Alabama, in 1922, a painful tooth extraction she endured as a child motivated her to go into dentistry. She did her undergraduate work at Tennessee A & I, received her doctorate in dental science (DDS) from Meharry in 1946 and, in 1948 became the first Black woman to earn a master's degree in public health from the University of Michigan. She went home to Birmingham, where she had a private practice and consulted for the county health department. "But I continued to find many people with problems that were due to an ignorance of dental health," she told a reporter in 1978.

Citing the shortage of dentists serving the Black community, only about one dentist for every 12,000 Black people compared to one for every 1,200 whites, Mobley stated, "I believe my call was to train more dentists." So, in 1957, she joined the Meharry faculty.

As Mobley told the reporter, "A dentist has to know everything that is happening to the patient and his body—what drugs he takes, any diseases he has had, and medications prescribed for them." In short, dentists have "total responsibility" for the care of their patients, she said.

A fellow of the American College of Dentists, the American Public Health Association and the Royal Society for the Promotion of Health, Mobley also had authored several articles for state and national dental journals on social and economic contributors to periodontal disease among young Blacks in low-income neighborhoods, and dental programs for chronically ill and elderly people. She would go on to serve, from 1978 to 1983, as the first female dean of Meharry's School of Dentistry, and later as the first female vice president of Meharry Medical College.

Eugenia Mobley, DDS, MPH

Mother was thrilled by what she saw and heard that day and enthusiastically accepted Mobley's offer. At the age of 48, Dr. Margaret Jones Chanin would at last begin her career.

Or maybe not.

At the beginning of the 1965-66 school year, Bob and I were taking a typing class together when suddenly he seemed to pass out and slid out of his chair onto the floor. His arms were flailing, and his legs were kicking uncontrollably. It was very scary. I rushed over to him, kneeled, and tried to hold him. I didn't know what else to do. The other students stood around us, silent and stupefied by what they were witnessing, while the teacher went to get help. The episode lasted only a couple of minutes. By the time she returned with the vice principal, the convulsions had stopped, and Bob started to come to.

"Oh my God!" he exclaimed. "My head is killing me. It feels like it's about to split wide open!"

Then, looking around, he realized he was on the floor, and everyone was standing around him, looking at him with astonished expressions on their faces.

"What happened?" he asked.

"You had a seizure, Robert," the teacher said. "We've called your mother. She's on her way to pick you up. You will need to see a doctor right away."

My brother was diagnosed with epilepsy. Fortunately, several anti-seizure drugs were on the market, and Bob was placed on a combination that kept his seizures in check. However, because of his medical condition, Mother and Dad were advised to transfer him to the Peabody College Demonstration School across 21st Avenue from Vanderbilt University so that he could receive more personal attention. He was not particularly happy about that, especially since, as a transfer student, he was not eligible to play on the basketball team. But he worked hard and made the team the fall of his senior year.

I played tennis and ran track in the spring, but basketball was my best sport. After my sophomore year at West End High School, I considered transferring to Montgomery Bell Academy, the exclusive, all-male private school a block from our home. But I liked the coed environment at West and I wanted to continue playing basketball at a high school that had won four Tennessee state basketball championships. I also wanted to play for the legendary Coach Joe Shapiro, who had taken West's Blue Jays to its most recent state championship in 1954.

In the fall of 1965, the beginning of my senior year, our team struggled—by December we had a 2-4 record. As January began, we beat Hume Fogg, starting us on a streak where we won 16 of our next 18 games. We upset Father Ryan on its home court for the first time in six years, winning by a score of 52-50. I missed my first free throw but hit my next 10, scoring 14 points. On January 15, Tennessean sportswriter Jimmy Davy wrote, "West's amazing Blue

Jays, who must have received a winning formula in their stockings during the Christmas holidays, captured their fourth straight victory last night with a resounding 58-49 decision over East's cold Eagles."

On March 9, we played Cameron High School, the first "all-Negro" boys' team to play in the regional tournament, which had just opened that year to Black schools. The Cameron players were physically imposing and were predicted to win by 20 points. We beat them in overtime, 39-38, playing what Davy called "a tantalizingly slow offense against the run-and-shoot Panthers."

Davy quoted Coach Shapiro as saying, "Until tonight I had never seen Cameron play a basketball game. But I knew they were taller, faster, and much stronger than us on the boards. That meant we had to hold the ball and make them over-anxious," he smiled.

"We wanted 'em to be in a big hurry when they finally got the ball—that's where the mistakes begin."

Unfortunately, our season ended in the next round of the regional tournament in the Vanderbilt gymnasium, as we lost to Stratford, 55-44. Coach Shapiro was as gracious as ever. "This is the finest bunch of boys I've ever had," he told us, as he told every team he ever coached.

Philip (center) was a starting player on West End High's 1965-1966 basketball team.

Besides basketball and keeping up with my studies, I did some college shopping during my senior year. I was a finalist for a National Merit Scholarship, but I needed a scholarship or financial aid. I wanted to attend a college with a good premed program where I also could play basketball. That fall, a graduate of Amherst College in western Massachusetts called my high school guidance counselor to ask if she knew of any seniors who might be interested in his alma mater. She gave him my name, and he put me in touch with a medical resident at Vanderbilt who had played basketball and baseball at Amherst. After talking to him, I decided to apply. Amherst offered me a scholarship if I committed to enroll in the fall—what they called Early Decision. I didn't hesitate. Come the fall of 1966, I would be an Amherst man.

My decision, and seeing how well Bob was doing, seemed to calm Mother down. She had asked Mobley if she could have a few months to make the necessary arrangements with her family. On May 1, 1966, buoyed by Dad's unflagging encouragement, she accepted Meharry's offer wholeheartedly. A few days later, about the time I graduated from high school, Mother began her career as Assistant Professor in the Department of Preventive Dentistry and Community Health, and as Assistant Director of the Oral Cancer Detection Program.

A speakerphone was installed at her desk so she wouldn't have to pick up the receiver with her prosthesis. She taught a preventive dentistry seminar to junior dental students and a class in community health to dental hygiene students. But most of her time was spent scheduling visits to local companies and nursing homes to promote oral cancer awareness and follow-up visits with patients. Her salary was $14,000 a year, more than six times the amount she made the previous year as a substitute teacher, earning $18 an hour. But I do believe Mother would have done the work for free.

"Dear Friends," she began her typewritten Christmas letter in 1966, "don't get out the eraser! Imagine, the Chanins at the same address for the 4th Christmas, just add the zip 37205!

"1966 has been a year with many changes ... the biggest change brought about by the end of Margaret's 20-year maternity leave! On May 1st she joined the staff at Meharry Dental College as Assistant Director of the program 'Dental Care for the Chronically Ill and Aged.' It has been a challenge and a joy to get back to dentistry."

One thousand miles from turbulent Nashville, on a leafy New England campus, I was undergoing a much different transformation. My parents were loyal Republicans. They'd voted for Eisenhower for president in 1952 and again in 1956, Nixon in 1960 and Goldwater in 1964. Now I was on the other side of the political spectrum. This was Kennedy country. My classmates hailed from every corner of the globe. I learned more from them than I did in any of my classes. The experience was exhilarating. I loved every minute of it.

During my first three months at college, I would walk to the Baptist Church on Sunday mornings. After all, I'd been raised as a Southern Baptist. Wednesday night church suppers, prayer meetings, singing in youth choirs, emotional revival meetings—these were all an integral part of my childhood, as was the faith that there was a God who answered prayers. The summer after high school, I worked as a door-to-door Bible salesman for the Southwestern Company to cover tuition for my first semester of college.

It didn't take me long to realize that I was the only Amherst College freshman who was rolling out of bed early on Sunday mornings to go to church. By December, like everybody else, I decided to sleep in. My beliefs had not changed but going to church had become less important.

Amherst was a men's college; women students would not be admitted until 1975. But two prestigious women's colleges, Smith and Mt. Holyoke, were within 10 miles of the campus. During my undergraduate years, my roommate and I ran the Amherst College sports news service. A half dozen classmates reported on the games and other sporting events; we'd edit them and send them on to the *Hartford Courant, Boston Globe*—even the *New York Times*.

Considering Grandmother's love of journalism, I guess my apple didn't fall far from her tree.

Chapter Thirteen
Open a Door

In February 1967 Judy Thurman, a reporter for *The Tennessean*, was assigned to cover a seminar on human relations hosted by the Nashville YWCA that featured Meharry surgeon Dr. Dorothy Brown, a clinical professor of surgery at Meharry and chief surgeon at Nashville's Riverside Hospital, who the previous fall had become the first Black woman elected to the Tennessee General Assembly. As a child, Brown said she was ashamed because she knew nothing about the history of her people. The only picture of a Black person she saw in a book on American history at school was that of a "buxom Negro woman" with a basket of cotton on her head. For many years Brown was frustrated and angry. But now, she said, "I feel blessed with the opportunity to be here and say to you, 'Come, let us reason together.'"

In her later years, Brown would receive a Human Relations Award from the National Conference of Christians and Jews, and a Carnegie Foundation humanitarian award. She died in 2004 at the age of 90.

While Brown spoke forcefully about the need for social change, Meharry continued to focus on its mission, demanding excellence from the doctors and dentists it trained while exerting a quiet pressure on the levers of power in its community. Among those who lectured regularly to Meharry students were prominent civil rights attorneys Avon Williams Jr. and his mentor, Z. Alexander Looby.

As a member of Nashville's city council since 1951, Looby had earned broad respect for his carefully reasoned arguments and balanced positions. In 1965, he worked with the Rev. Kelly Miller Smith, who had helped organize Nashville's lunch-counter demonstrations, Rabbi Randall Falk, a leader of Nashville's Jewish community, and Meharry radiology professor Dr. Edwin Mitchell to establish Nashville's first Human Relations Commission. "The idea," Looby was fond of saying, "is to open a door without breaking it down."

That was Mother's approach too. She changed people's perceptions of those with disabilities merely by her physical presence. Statuesque and beautiful, confident but not callous, proud but not preening, she exuded charm and elegance. She was somebody you wanted to get to know, somebody you would listen to and take seriously. That was Mother's version of changing attitudes, through one-on-one interactions, and that's why, I believe, she was a good fit for Meharry.

In April, Thurman asked Mother if she could interview her for a feature to be published during National Handicapped Week. Mother agreed. The resulting story was entitled "Loss of arms inconvenient—but not incapacitating."

"If you have drive and ambition before you have a terrible accident like I had, then you will be able to adjust afterwards," Mother told Thurman. Of course, there are days when she's down, "but everyone has those days," she said.

Mother credited Dad, as she always did, with helping her to become more independent. "My husband says his only hobby is keeping me in operation," she laughed.

Much of her work was done using the latest in conference phones—no dialing required. With the clamp at the end of her prosthesis she simply picked up a dowel stick, punched a button on the phone and started talking. "These conference phones were the best things invented for people like me," she said.

As director of the oral community control clinic, one of her responsibilities was to encourage the dental students always to educate their patients in good oral hygiene—including frequent brushing and flossing. "Don't put all this expensive hardware in their mouths," she'd tell the students, "and then not tell 'em how to take care of it!"

Mother's position also involved counseling indigent patients. "After a person has received his new teeth, he is sometimes sent down here to learn how to take care of them and adjust to them," she told Thurman. "Or, if he needs surgery, I try to convince him he should not be afraid and he should try to save his teeth."

Thurman concluded: "After talking with Margaret and seeing how well she manages despite her 'inconvenience,' it is doubtful that the patients remain afraid of needed dental work. In fact, they probably leave the office a little embarrassed they every complained about it in the first place."

In the spring of 1967, demonstrations against the Vietnam War were gathering steam across the country. So were calls from the growing Black Power movement to confront more directly the rise in racially motivated acts of violence. Among those who advocated a more aggressive response was Stokely Carmichael, then chair of the Student Nonviolent Coordinating Committee (SNCC). Emerging from the student-led sit-ins at segregated lunch counters in Nashville and Greensboro, North Carolina, SNCC was becoming more militant as the turbulent and traumatic '60s unfolded.

Tall and handsome, Carmichael was wildly popular with his audiences. His speeches were fierce, entertaining, and so often confrontational that his SNCC associates started calling him the "Magnificent Barbarian."

That spring the students at Vanderbilt University invited Carmichael to participate in their annual Impact Symposium alongside a wildly diverse group of speakers that included the Rev. Martin Luther King, Jr., Strom Thurman, the U.S. Senator from South Carolina known for his opposition to Civil Rights legislation, and "beat" poet Allen Ginsberg. Carmichael's invitation drew immediate fire from Vanderbilt trustees, including James Stahlman, publisher of the city's conservative afternoon newspaper, the *Nashville Banner*. The state Senate passed a resolution calling Carmichael a "dangerous, unprincipled demagogue." But Vanderbilt Chancellor Alexander Heard stood firm in support of his students. They had invited Carmichael and would not be denied.

Carmichael delivered three addresses during his visit to Nashville, the first on Thursday, April 6, at Fisk University. "You've been brainwashed to believe this country is white," he admonished his audience. "You don't have the guts to stand up and say, 'We are black ... and we are beautiful.'" The next day at Tennessee State University, he urged the crowd of well over 1,000 people to organize and "take over this city."

Carmichael was more subdued when he spoke in Vanderbilt's Memorial Auditorium on Saturday afternoon. "Our Negro communities can become either concentration camps filled with miserable people who have only the power to destroy," he said, "or they can become organized communities that make a meaningful contribution to the nation." King, who concluded the symposium, was more forceful. "There is nothing more dangerous than the man who feels he has no status," he warned. "As long as justice for all people is postponed, there will continue to be riots."

For many in Nashville's Black community, King and Carmichael's messages resonated deeply. Three months earlier, the Sixth Circuit Court of Appeals in Cincinnati had ruled against a citizens group that claimed the proposed route of the Interstate 40 highway through the middle of North Nashville's Black community would do irreparable harm. The group's prediction was correct. Many neighborhood businesses were forced to close when the highway project, which began in 1968, cut them off from their customers. Home values dropped by more than 30 percent. Nashville was not alone. Across the country in the 1960s and early 1970s, interstate highway construction and "urban renewal" projects drew a line directly through neighborhoods of color, leaving residents feeling hurt, abandoned, and powerless.

Eventually, long-simmering resentments, even in peaceful, "get-along" Nashville, reached a boiling point. On Saturday evening, following King's address at Vanderbilt, the manager of a white-owned restaurant on Jefferson Street called police to eject a drunken patron. Their arrival set off a spontaneous riot near the Fisk campus, with roving bands of students throwing rocks, bricks, and bottles at police throughout the night. A Fisk student was shot in the leg.

The next night the rioting resumed at TSU. Molotov cocktails were thrown through the windows of several small businesses, including a barbershop, a gas station, and a liquor store. The melee continued until the rioters were dispersed by tear gas. No one was killed but dozens were injured including a student who was shot in the neck. Thirty-six people were arrested, among them 11 students from TSU and two from Fisk.

Tennessee Governor Buford Ellington and state Education Commissioner J. Howard Warf blamed outside agitators for the rioting and pledged to deal with the "black power problem" at TSU. Student leaders responded that the problem was not Black power; meager state appropriations made it difficult for the university to recruit qualified instructors or maintain campus services and facilities. State officials were not persuaded. Eventually, they forced the university to expel the students who had been arrested and limited out-of-state admissions. By the end of 1967 TSU's president, Walter S. Davis, had left office due to an undisclosed illness. An interim faculty committee would run the university during the search for his successor.

That spring, Granddad's sturdy, brave heart began to fail. Nine times, in 1967, Mother drove to the hospital in Osceola to spend time with him. At one point, Grandmother penned this handwritten note to her family in Nashville: "One night I was reading the paper and had the curtain drawn part way and light dimmed for him to go to sleep (he couldn't see me) and he began to pray, such a sweet prayer, thanking 'Our Father' for letting him live 87-and-a-half years, for such a nice family, good children, and 'I'm sure you will let me live another year or two.'"

That was not to be. On June 13, 1967, at the age of 87, this cheerful farmer who had encouraged the women in his life to become all that they could be, and who loved them fiercely and completely, left this world to meet his Maker. He was laid to rest in Pleasant Hill Cemetery in Brunswick, Tennessee, where his parents, grandparents, and three sisters had been buried before him. His obituary in *The Osceola Times* ended with the English poet John Oxenham's "After Work:"

Lord, when Thou seest that my work is done,
Let me not linger on,
With failing powers,
Adown the weary hours, —

A workless worker in a world of work.
But, with a word,
Just bid me home,
And I will come
Right gladly, —
Yea, right gladly
Will I come.

Bob later wrote of his grandfather, "He modeled for me that humility which brings power and love and respect into one's life. When he died, he was the oldest living deacon in his church. Both Black and white mourned his death. I was 16 and knew that a great man had passed away."

In the fall, Mother and Dad moved out of the bottom-floor apartment they'd been renting since we moved to Nashville in 1963 and bought a three-bedroom, 2,000-square-foot house down the street at 3810 Richland Avenue for $15,500. It's the same house I live in today.

They were able to buy the house because of a settlement Mother received from the Houston Lighting and Power Company in 1941. She'd sued the company, alleging it was responsible for her boyfriend's death and the loss of her arms because it had allowed its power line to sag dangerously low over the bay where they were sailing. She used the settlement to buy stock in the company. Over the years, the stock split and doubled. Whenever Mother had a significant expense, she'd sell shares of her stock.

At the end of 1967, it appeared that Dad was finally getting the recognition he deserved. Over the years, he'd authored or co-authored several scientific papers, some of which had been published in prestigious journals including *Science*. In December, he was notified that in recognition of his significant contributions to the field of chemistry, he had been elected a life member of a premier scientific society, the American Association for the Advancement of Science.

Like liquid on a Bunsen burner, however, Dad's high spirits soon evaporated. A scant three months later, on March 26, 1968, he received a letter from Dr. William M. Jackson, dean of the faculty of arts and sciences at TSU and a member of the interim committee running the university, notifying him that his contract as Associate Professor of Chemistry would not be renewed in the fall. Jackson noted low ratings that Dad had received since he joined the faculty four years earlier: "inclined to create friction—does not get along well; shows tendency to react impulsively and without restraint; is inflexible and intolerant."

In what would become a very public row, Dad and four other faculty members who were dismissed or demoted that year said they had been dealt with unjustly by the university's administration. They accused the university of engaging in "irregular procedures" and disregarding professional ethics. Jackson told the *Tennessean* the actions were justified and enumerated the low ratings spelled out in his letter to Dad.

Dad retorted, in a subsequent newspaper article, that he was fired because the administration was suppressing dissent among its faculty. He said he had repeatedly complained about poor maintenance, inadequate supplies and equipment, and other problems at the university.

"It's very difficult to get equipment and chemicals that are needed," he told the *Tennessean*. "You send in an order, and it is never filled. You ask what happened to it and they say it was lost. I have complained about the maintenance. Wastebaskets are not emptied. Floors are not swept. Windows are not washed, and the air conditioning is horrible … The only way to get anything at the school is to complain. I refused to sit still. I complained and made waves and that's why I'm on my way out."

At a national level, 1968 was married by tragedy, death, and violence. On April 4, the day after delivering his now-famous "I've Been to the Mountaintop" speech, the Rev. Martin Luther King Jr. was standing on the balcony of his room at the Lorraine Motel in Memphis when an assassin's bullet took his life. Two months later, on June 5, Bobby Kennedy, who had just won the California primary in his campaign to succeed Lyndon Johnson as president, was also gunned down in a crowded kitchen hallway at the Ambassador Hotel in Los Angeles. Later that summer, the televised conflagration between anti-war protesters and police at the Democratic National Convention in Chicago helped propel Republican Richard Nixon to the White House in November.

But it was King's death in April that set off a convulsion of riots across the country. In north Nashville, near the corner of Jefferson Street and 18th

Avenue North, dozens of people threw rocks at passing cars, and some fired guns. Several area businesses were burned and looted. Governor Ellington called up 4,000 National Guard troops. Tanks rumbled down Broadway, in front of the Parthenon in Centennial Park and down the narrow streets around the Fisk University campus.

The rioting continued into Friday, April 5. Nashville Mayor Beverly Briley ordered a curfew that forced Nashville's signature country music venue, the Grand Ole Opry, at the time located in the red-bricked Ryman Auditorium a block off Broadway, to cancel a performance for the first time in 43 years. Early Saturday, about 175 National Guardsman were called to the TSU campus after a sniper fired on police. No one was wounded but officers ordered students out of their dormitory rooms at gunpoint, hands held high, as they searched unsuccessfully for the gunman. Hours later, guardsmen in gas masks and armed with tear gas were still patrolling the area. As the violence subsided and the Guardsmen began to leave the city, the curfew was lifted—nine days later.

Dad's complaints about his employer were echoed a month later in a class-action lawsuit aimed at stopping the planned $4.2 million expansion of the University of Tennessee adult higher education center in Nashville into a four-year institution. The lawsuit, in which Governor Ellington was the lead defendant, alleged that the state's plan would frustrate efforts by TSU to attract more white students, further marginalizing the predominantly Black university and jeopardizing its future. After winding through the courts for several years, the litigation ultimately led to a merger: UT-Nashville became part of TSU.

Dad's public airing of shortages and shortcomings on the TSU campus probably strengthened the university's case against the UT-Nashville expansion. Yet he would continue to be dogged by his reputation as a troublemaker. For several months after his separation from TSU, he tried unsuccessfully to find another teaching position in Nashville. He finally settled for a research position in the Department of Oral Pathology at Meharry. It was, he joked in the family's annual Christmas letter, "very conveniently located down the hall from Margaret. Remains to be seen whether this will be an advantage or disadvantage."

This time, however, Dad's humor had a hard edge to it.

Chapter Fourteen
Such a Time as This

In stark contrast to the violence that flared in Nashville and throughout the country in 1968 and Dad's humiliation at work, Mother's experiences were increasingly liberating. Outside of her work at Meharry, she served on the Board of Directors of the American Cancer Society of Davidson County and was a member of several professional organizations. She volunteered for Outlook Nashville, a non-profit agency that had been established along with Goodwill Industries of Middle Tennessee in 1957. Its mission was to help people with disabilities find employment, and to educate society at large to "focus on the person, not the handicap."

In May 1968, Mother was interviewed by Ida Clemons, a reporter for the *Commercial Appeal,* while attending the Tennessee State Dental Association meeting in Memphis.

"I'm very happy and feel that I'm making a contribution to dentistry," she told Clemons. "Last week we found the eighth patient with cancer. We have picked up several pre-cancerous lesions and it is exciting to feel you are doing even a small part in finding these very early so the patients can get prompt treatment."

As she became more established in her job, Mother often would travel alone to represent Meharry at dental meetings. Accompanying her on one of those trips, her long-time friend and former speech teacher Sara Lowrey observed that "when she registered in the hotel, she took the pen between her teeth and signed the register, then asked if someone could help her get to bed and dressed the next morning. When she met her fellow dentists in the lobby … she said to one, 'May I have dinner with you, and will you feed me?'" As it was with her fellow students in dental school more than 20 years before, her new acquaintances always seemed honored to be asked.

In the spring of 1968, Mother was informed that she had been selected as one of three "Women of Achievement" to be honored at a banquet hosted by the Business and Professional Women's Club of Nashville.

She nearly refused the honor. "You can understand that it isn't pleasant to have one's handicaps discussed in public and in print," she told club official Earline Rogers. "But I always feel that in turning down such offers, I might miss an opportunity to encourage someone who needs encouragement. So, I'll be your candidate."

Prior to the banquet, Rogers interviewed Mother in our home to gather material for her remarks. I was still at Amherst, finishing up my sophomore year, but Bob, who was about to graduate from Peabody Demonstration School, told Rogers that he was looking forward to going to Baylor University, Mother's alma mater, in the fall.

The banquet was held on May 23 at the historic Hermitage Hotel, two blocks from the state Capitol.

In her introductory remarks, Rogers said she came away from interviewing Mother "with a definite impression of having been in a place filled with love, understanding, faith in God and dedication to service."

Was the tragedy that befell Mother a mere random event, or was there some purpose to it? "Perhaps," Rogers said, "the answer is found in the Bible."

She turned to the story of Esther, the Jewish queen of a Persian ruler who, when urged by Mordecai, intercedes to save her people from destruction. "Who knoweth," Mordecai said to Esther, "whether thou art come to the kingdom for such a time as this?"

Looking up from her notes, Rogers smiled and looked over at Mother, who was seated at the table closest to the lectern. "Who knows," she said, "that this strikingly attractive, brilliant woman was not chosen through her own tragedy to bring comfort and hope to all handicapped persons?"

The summer of 1968, after my sophomore year at Amherst College, I flew to Honolulu, Hawaii, where I worked as a parking lot attendant during the evenings. In the mornings and early afternoons, I'd be on Waikiki Beach. During my off hours, I also read two influential works by psychoanalyst Erich Fromm, *The Art of Loving* and *The Dogma of Christ*. From the first, I encountered the concept of self-love—the essential quality of respecting and knowing myself as a prerequisite to being able to truly love another. But the second, a socio-psychoanalytic examination of the evolution of Christian dogma from the early church to modern times, shook my faith to its core.

I flew home to Nashville at the end of the summer and experienced a depression that lasted for about three weeks. I was no longer certain about life. I mourned the death of a belief system to which I could no longer subscribe. I would attend my mother's church, Immanuel Baptist on Belle Meade Boulevard, when I was home on vacations from college and graduate school, but I no longer believed most of what was said and sung there. It was clear to me that the tragedies and pain of the world were far too great to believe that there was a God who listened to people's prayers and intervened to make things right.

In the fall of 1968, two young Black men from Los Angeles arrived in Nashville to begin their first year at the Meharry School of Dentistry. Neither had been to the South before.

John E. Maupin Jr. and Rueben Warren would leave their mark on Meharry. But just as profoundly, Meharry would leave its mark on them. Among those who impacted them was a white faculty member who had lost both arms in a boating accident—Dr. Margaret Chanin.

"She taught me to go past a physical disability," said Maupin, who would go on to serve as president and CEO of Meharry Medical College from 1994 to 2006. "When you first see her, it's this lady with no arms. How is she going to teach dentistry? She didn't try to teach you clinical dentistry. She taught you the other parts of dentistry. But more importantly you just got past her disability ... At first you were taken aback, but it didn't take long before you didn't see it anymore ... She taught us, don't get blindsided by people's appearance or disabilities. Take people for who they are. She didn't lecture about that. It was her presence, how she carried herself that taught us."

"People always think dentists are doing something with their hands," added Warren, who succeeded Mobley as dean of the Meharry School of Dentistry in 1983. "She helped us to understand the broader domains of oral health. It's not all about drilling teeth ... Because of her physical challenges she was forced to use her mind in ways others didn't ... I was quite impressed with that.

"We never got a sense of condescension or paternalism from her," he said. "It was never that. It was always, 'I'm doing what I'm supposed to be doing ... I'm doing this because it's the right thing to do.' That gave me the strength and the confidence to know she's not doing me any favors. She's accomplishing *her* mission, in line with the mission of Meharry and the mission I wanted to pursue."

John E. Maupin, Jr., DDS, MBA   *Rueben C. Warren, DDS, MPH, DrPH, MDIV*

New Yorker Morgan Hines, who also began his dental training at Meharry in 1968, agreed. "She's doing her job ... without arms, and I'm sitting here complaining because I've got a practical (preclinical assessment) I've got to pass," recalled Hines, who later established his dentistry practice in Columbia, Tennessee. "If it was me, I would have given up. But once you realize what she has accomplished and the many students she has affected, then you say, 'Shoot, if she can do it, you can do it.'"

Mother, likely the only armless instructor of dentistry in the country, and Mobley, the second woman to serve as dean of a U.S. dental school, made quite a team. "I think they chose each other," Warren said, "two women in public health. There was a connection there."

Years after her death in 2011, Mobley's achievements continue to inspire. "She brought public health to dentistry," Warren said. "She had a vision that others couldn't see and the perseverance to see it through. I went on to do public health in large part because of that department. Dr. Mobley and Dr. Chanin and others taught me to 'see beyond the mouth.'"

Like Mobley and other members of Meharry's faculty, Mother urged her students to be the best they could be. 'The curriculum was intense," Maupin recalled. "The expectations were high." The instructors were out to "toughen up" their students, to prepare them for a future in health care that would not always be fair. "What they shared with us was, you're going to reach a world where there will be some prejudice against you," he said. "There are going to be some barriers that you're going to have to overcome. And you're going to have to overcome them with your excellence and your hard work and your work ethic. It's not enough to be smart. You have to have a good work ethic to go with it.

"It all had the same focus," Maupin continued. "We're going to train you to be the best dentist that's ever come out of a dental school ... and we're going to train you not only as good professionals but as good people, as good individuals. We're going to nurture you on the way."

Friends since college, Maupin and Warren were swept up in the anti-war protests and the Black Power movement of the mid-1960s. Maupin attended San Jose State, just south of San Francisco, while Warren went to San Francisco State, which was at the time, as he put it, "the most radical campus in the country." Student-run organizations including the Black Student Union, the Third World Liberation Front and Students for a Democratic Society held frequent sit-ins, marches and rallies and sometimes clashed violently with police. Social justice was part of Meharry's mission, too, but upon arrival in Nashville, the two young men from California quickly learned they had to be careful how they exercised their idealism.

In his senior year, Maupin went to the office of the Meharry president, Dr. Lloyd Elam, to tell him that his class wanted to host a representative of the Black Panther Party, a political organization that sponsored community service projects, but which also advocated class struggle against police brutality and other injustices.

"I hear what you're saying, and I don't agree," Elam told him. "I'm not going to let your classmates take over my office. Unless they don't want their degrees, then I think you better advise them."

Elam and many of his faculty members were concerned that hosting Black Panther activists would attract negative publicity, making it harder for Meharry to navigate the institutional barriers erected during the Jim Crow era. Elam's message to the students was quickly communicated.

"You had to appreciate they had to protect Meharry no matter what they believed or thought," Maupin said years later. "What was most important was protecting Meharry from outside issues that may damage our reputation, our funding, or our continued existence. At the same time what made the school have a great reputation was the success of its students. We were all very, very aware that wherever we went, we represented our institution and our race."

That didn't mean Meharry was totally closed to any sort of activism. On the contrary, Meharry students spent time with civil rights attorney Avon Williams and his mentor, Z. Alexander Looby, who lectured on medical jurisprudence. Under the supervision of Dr. Matthew Walker, students helped provide basic medical and dental services to Black patients in Mound Bayou, Mississippi, and Tuskegee, Alabama.

"All that was part of the Meharry experience," Warren said. "We were young and a little more radical than the school wanted us to be." But "Meharry was flexible enough to give us the space not to harm ourselves as students ... They gave us space to grow."

Of Mother, he said, "She *was* Meharry. You can be *at* Meharry and not be *of* Meharry. There's a difference ... Living with a disability allowed her to demonstrate that mission ... to reach those others couldn't reach. An instructor told me that Meharry takes students nobody wants, and four years later produces doctors and dentists everybody wants. It's true ... Meharry empowered me ... You leave with a responsibility to do the things that you know need to be done."

Warren earned his dental degree from Meharry in 1972, and later, a master's degree and doctorate from the Harvard School of Public Health, and a master's degree in divinity from the Interdenominational Theological Center in Atlanta, Georgia.

Dean of the Meharry School of Dentistry for five years, from 1983 to 1988, Warren subsequently served as associate director for minority health at the U.S. Centers for Disease Control and Prevention in Atlanta. He currently is director of the National Center for Bioethics in Research and Health Care and professor of bioethics at Tuskegee University.

Tuskegee was the site of the notorious "Study of Untreated Syphilis in the Negro Male." Beginning in 1932, and until news accounts exposed and shut down the study 40 years later, federal health officials recruited nearly 400 men with latent syphilis to investigate the natural history of the disease. The men were not told they would go untreated, even after penicillin became widely available in the late 1940s. Instead, they were told that they had "bad blood." By the time the study was halted in 1972, more than 100 of them had died from complications of the disease, 40 of their wives had been infected, and 19 children had been born with congenital syphilis, which can cause severe and permanent birth defects.

Through education and scholarship, the Tuskegee center's mission is to make sure that such an assault on the dignity, worth and lives of vulnerable human beings under the guise of medical "science" never happens again.

Maupin's path took him to Baltimore, where he earned an MBA at Loyola College. He went on to become deputy health commissioner for the City of Baltimore and CEO of a federally qualified community health center in Atlanta before taking the helm at Meharry. Later he served as president and CEO of the Morehouse School of Medicine in Atlanta. He retired in 2014.

Maupin's career path reflected what he learned at Meharry.

"Do right and do good, and you can also do well," he said. "... Do the best you can and try to make a difference, and it will get recognized. And then some doors will open, and you have to make your choices."

I can see Margaret Chanin's imprint on the lives of John Maupin and Rueben Warren. I'm sure of it, because Mother's "wide-open thinking" is a part of me, too.

Chapter Fifteen
There Must Be a Dawn

The months dragged on, and still Dad could not find a suitable position. The work in the oral pathology lab at Meharry was not satisfactory. One day he got mad at his boss and walked out, saying he would not return without an apology. The apology didn't come, and Dad was out of work—again. His demeanor darkened.

Then, in July 1969, he wandered into the kitchen where Mother was preparing dinner and blurted out what he'd been waiting for weeks to say.

"Margaret, there's nothing for me here. I'm leaving. I've asked my cousin Stella in Philadelphia, and she says I can stay with her for a while."

I wasn't there. I was home for the summer but was out with some of my high school friends when Dad decided to drop his bomb. Bob also was home after his first year at Baylor, but he had decided to take a break from college. He was working as an orderly at Central State, the state mental hospital in Nashville, and had gotten his own place. So, it was just Dad and Mother in the house on Richland Avenue.

It is hard for me to imagine the conversation. I had rarely seen my mother angry or overwrought. But if there were any time for her to be so, this was certainly the time.

"What do you mean, you're 'leaving?' What about me? Who is going to take care of me? How will I be able to manage on my own—without you?"

"I can't take it anymore," he mumbled. "I have to go."

While Dad was often disagreeable, he avoided direct, eyeball-to-eyeball confrontations. I imagine at this point he simply turned away, went to the bedroom, and closed the door behind him.

Mother may have tried to talk him out of leaving. I know that Bob and I certainly did. But it was no use. Within the week, Dad had packed his belongings into his VW bug, and had driven up to Philadelphia. The arrangement with his cousin didn't last long, however. Stella Chanin rented out her bedrooms to students from the Philadelphia College of Osteopathy. In late August, after a few weeks of sharing a bathroom with strangers, Dad decided to return to his parents' house in Union, New Jersey.

He'd visited his folks over the years, of course, but usually with us in tow. This was the first time, since he left for college 31 years before, that he came back on his own—to stay. It was as if he'd forgotten why he left in the first place. His father was an unrelentingly critical man, and that trait had only hardened with age. I can only imagine what the discussions must have been like around the Chanin dinner table.

"I told you so," the elder Chanin might have said. "You should have stayed here, opened a drug store like I told you to. You could've made a good living for yourself, married a nice Jewish girl. Instead, look at you now! What do you have to show for yourself after 30 years? My two grandsons, yes. But what else? Nothing!"

Dad, his face reddening, probably stammered a response, and no doubt tried to justify his decisions and his life, but not very convincingly, not even to himself. Finally, he threw his napkin onto his plate, angrily scraped his chair against the linoleum floor of the kitchen and stormed out into the night. Perhaps he escaped to a neighborhood bar to drink away his disappointment and his bitterness. Dad never drank to excess. Despite his many character flaws, he remained a careful man. After a couple of hours, he probably returned to his parents' darkened house, used his own key to get in the backdoor, treaded as lightly as he could up the hall to his bedroom, shook off his clothes, put on his pajamas, slipped into bed, and glared into the darkness until sleep overcame him.

And what about Mother? She had lost her main support system, the man who for 25 years had encouraged her and cared for her in the most intimate ways. But she'd known profound loss before. She'd lost her arms, the hands with which she had fed and bathed and dressed herself and combed her hair. Just as in 1941, she had to dig deep. She made do. She arranged for women to come to the house to bathe and dress and feed her. It wasn't easy. When she couldn't find anyone to feed her, there were times when she had to pour her meal into a bowl, lean over it and lap it up like a dog.

What Mother had, and what Dad did not, was faith. She leaned on it. Rather than allow the darkness to swallow her up, as my father unfortunately had, she focused on the light, the goodness that emanated from the center of her life. She was grateful for it, cheerful even, for she knew that God would not abandon her. He would see her through. She knew outsiders considered her to be a Pollyanna, unflaggingly optimistic even while staring tragedy in the face. But her good spirits were not for show. She truly believed things would work out the way they were supposed to.

"When things happen to us, God gives us the courage to go on," she told a church audience in 1973. "We must take care that we are not over-concerned over our future, our protection, or our security, and we must not get so bound up in our lives that there is no place for faith." That doesn't mean Dad hadn't broken her heart. It doesn't mean she never cried. She just kept the brokenness and the tears to herself, revealing them only on occasion to those closest to her, including the man she would always love.

In September 1969, Mother wrote Dad an apparent response to a previous letter from him. I found the correspondence among her papers. I don't know if she sent the letter to him. If she did, he must have he returned it to her. Because it is so revealing, I include the letter here just as she typed it, with a few comments of mine in italics. I can see Mother laboriously hunting and pecking one typewriter key at a time with a pencil clenched in her teeth. Dated September 5 it begins, "Dearest Marty."

"While the clothes are washing and the skillet is soaking, I'll endeavor to ans. some of your questions. Bob has just left to spend the night at his apt, as he has to report in at 6:45 at Central State (nursing dir. asked him to work for which he will get paid overtime as he was due to be off). This week and next week he is working the dayshift as the orientation classes meet from 12 to 4.

"Lynn (*a friend of Bob's*) dropped by and fed, undressed me and helped with the dishes, she will be back about 10:30 to spend the night. (*Lynn's parents*) are out of town for a car meet until next Sat. so she will stay with me or I'll stay over there.

"I had room all ready and was to have moved a girl in Wed. whom Phil and I had interviewed on the 28th (Residence for Young Women on Blair) alas she called on Tues. night that she couldn't come. The social worker indicated that I was lucky!

"I have really covered the waterfront, my phone bill will be like the nat. debt as I had authorized Mrs. Morris to call student in L.A. and later one in N.C. to ones that had been accepted and then asked to withdraw for financial reasons. Last nite I authorized Supt. of Orphanage in Franklin to call girl in Paris, Tenn. who will be in Belmont this fall to see if she is interested. At this point it is a good thing that I'm a Pollyanna.

"Yes, Bob still goes to Meharry (*possibly for treatment for his epilepsy or for counseling*). I think she has helped him a great deal or at least something has. He was up at 5 this morning showered us both, helped with breakfast, dressed me and was on his way at 7 with nary a complaint!

"The night before we were up til 1 and got up at 4 in order to get Phil out for 7:40 flight (*back to college*). I called your Mother just as we were loading the car, sorry things are so sticky there. Your Mother tells me she is losing weight (*due to the conflict between father and son*) but what a hell of a way to lose it!

"I think Phil will go to N.Y. tonight or tomorrow, visit a day or 2 and wait for Chip to arrive then they will drive on up to Amherst. Phil sold his coins, all but the Indian Heads, on Wed. for $88 so this is what he took with him. We contemplated selling your stamps but he thought they were too beautiful to part with ...

"I spent nearly an hour with Val (*their attorney*) today. What do you mean 'My hands are tied til status settled legally?' Val says that a legal separation is purely for determining support, just as I related to you earlier. If you want things legal and we have to go to all the technicality it would seem that a divorce is the wisest. This can be done for about $200 and we do not have to be in a hurry to pay it. Is this what you want? If so, what grounds do you prefer me to use? Desertion requires that you will be away a year. The other choice is cruel and inhumane treatment which requires 2 witness that can testify that this is so. Whoever we'd use would require them to lie since this is not the case. One can begin to see why there is a movement on foot to correct these laws.

"Bob ... seems to be very happy in the work, but the pay is only 275, he has applied to attend a 3 mos. aide school which would raise him to 320 on completion. He passed the Civil Service test and received a form to have Goldner (*his doctor*) fill out concerning the epilepsy. Anyhow he plans on trying to hold 2 jobs, if not at P.O. he wants me to inquire about having a aide or orderly at Meharry!

"Sister arrived from Ga. On Friday AM and left Mon., was ill the whole time ...

"You asked for a list of expenses:

House payment--------121.00 – Taxes & ins. ave. $25 per mo.
Bank notes --------------154.00
G.M.A.C.-----------------114.00
VW -----------------------72.00
Car insurance ----------15.00 monthly ave. (this mo. And 2 more of &54)
Boys (*car insurance*)---25.00
   (*Penciled total 511.00*)
"The following are monthly averages from '68
Utilities------------------$75.00
Medical ------------------125.00
Prof. exp. ----------------50.00
Help ----------------------56.00
   (*Penciled 511 + 306 = 817*)

"If something doesn't break pretty soon to take up the slack that the boys were providing I don't know what we are going to do.

"I tried to change my dependents to 2, was sure I checked zero but found out they were withholding on basis of 2 already so thought best not to alter it as we surely don't want to send in taxes.

"If at all possible I'd like to remain in this house so I would not have to pay rent of at least 150 and then would not have taxes and interest to deduct and we'd be right back where we started at 3822 (*their previous address on Richland Avenue*), nor am I sure I could sell it for enough to pay off mortgage and bank notes. I don't think I could take on a move plus trying to find someone to stay with me and still do justice to my job—haven't really earned my pay this week!

"Better say goodnight, keep on keeping on, there must be a dawn.

"We picked up another ca.pt. (*oral cancer patient in the Meharry clinic*) today, makes 2 since July 1.

"I called VW credit mgr.,explained that we'd pay when we could and not to report us as bad risks ...

"The bathroom leaks in boy's bath so bad that I'm not going to pay Wehby (*the plumber*) even if I could until something done, even closet floor in back room moldy!

"So much for the sad saga at 3810 ... (*signed in pencil*) "Mgt"

Why did he do it? Why did Dad leave her? At last Mother was engaged in a fulfilling career. While she was not as dependent upon him as she had been, he could have stayed—should have stayed—by her side while waiting for another position. That's what many of today's men would do. But times were different then. It would have threatened the masculinity of most traditional men of that era to stay home and "keep house," even for a short time. As I came to realize years later, at his core, Dad was not only a traditional man; he was also very insecure. Was he a narcissist?

In Greek mythology, Narcissus falls in love with his own reflection in a pool of water. Unable to pull himself away, he eventually dies from starvation. Likewise, a narcissistic personality disorder is a mental condition characterized by a deep need for excessive attention and a lack of empathy for others. Beneath an inflated sense of their own importance and a mask of extreme confidence, however, narcissists have a fragile self-esteem that is vulnerable to the slightest criticism. They are so demanding of attention that they can suck the air out of a room, leaving others in their midst feeling empty and not knowing why. Eventually, if narcissists feel they are not being given enough of the attention and admiration they believe they deserve, they may become unhappy, disappointed, and even angry. They may, like Dad did, just up and leave even the most committed relationships, looking for greener and more satisfying pastures elsewhere.

Dr. Bruce Richards, who grew up across the street from us in Florence, Alabama, and who later reestablished a decades-long friendship with Mother in Nashville, doesn't think that was the case.

"Narcissists know they're assholes," he said. "They just don't care. I didn't get that from Marty at all. I remember as a child having trouble reading him. My mother described him as odd, but she and my dad had a great deal of admiration for him, for his compassion. He made quite a number of sacrifices for Margaret. He was probably somebody that we would call on the 'spectrum' now—like Asperger's syndrome—somebody who didn't pick up on conventional social cues very easily. Without Margaret, it's pretty hard to imagine that he would have had a family life or a social life or the ability to interact with the public at all. Margaret made him OK."

He's right. Mother told me that when she and Dad went out socially, she'd keep her ear cocked to his conversation, even across the room. If he "put his foot in his mouth," she'd walk over and in her engaging, sparkling manner, set things right.

I suppose that the events of 1968 in Nashville had become too much for my father to handle. As far as I know he, like my mother and her parents, was colorblind. The color of one's skin simply didn't make any difference to them. That doesn't mean they were oblivious to what was going on in the world around them. Both my parents worked in predominantly Black institutions. Unlike most other white people in Nashville at the time, they saw and heard and felt firsthand the racial tensions that seemed to be ripping apart the world around them.

Dad also had a heightened and very rigidly applied sense of right and wrong. In 1948, he had been unfairly vilified as a communist for supporting Henry Wallace's Quixotic bid for the presidency. Eleven years later, he was let go from another job when he refused to change failing grades so his students wouldn't lose their eligibility to play collegiate football. Now this. The ground was crumbling beneath his feet. He was let go once again. He had lost once again. One can only take so much loss, especially if one has nothing to hold on to.

I have no doubt that Dad loved Mother until the day he died. He was the one who had encouraged her all these years, who had in so many ways made it possible for her to achieve as much as she did. He could have—should have—been proud of that, and grateful. What a wonderful life he'd had. Yet because of his deep-seated insecurity and, yes, his personality disorder, Dad never could reach that place of peace, sufficiency, and wholeness that Mother had found and freely shared with everyone in her life.

"That's the tragedy of the whole thing," Mother told an interviewer in 1997. "He was so bright and had such opportunities. If only he had not been reared in a dysfunctional family. He had a lot of emotional problems."

By October, three months after he moved in with his parents in New Jersey, he and Grandfather weren't on speaking terms. So, Dad called me up.

"Can I move in with you, in the dorm?"

I shared a suite with three roommates. Each of us had a bedroom; we shared a bathroom, and a common area with the TV and a couch. I wasn't very good with boundaries in those days. "Sure," I said, albeit a bit half-heartedly. In a very co-dependent fashion, I gave him my room and started sleeping on the couch.

I got him an interview with the head of the Chemistry Department at Amherst College, who hired him to mix chemical compounds. Then he moved into a little rooming house called the Friendly Door. He gave me his VW bug because he could walk from the Friendly Door to work. Of course, he got to know my roommates. At lunchtime, he'd come down to the dining hall where I was bussing tables to cover my college expenses, and he'd chat with my friends.

Just before Christmas, he moved back into my dorm room, and told me he'd decided. He was going to immigrate to Israel to start a new life. He could get a job as a chemist in the country's booming textile industry. He didn't know much Hebrew, but he could speak German—he'd taken some courses in college. There were a lot of German Jews in Israel, survivors of the Holocaust.

On January 2, 1970, Dad boarded a plane bound for Tel Aviv. As suddenly as he had reentered my life, he left it again. Frankly, I was relieved. But I was worried, too.

Not about him. Mostly I worried about Mother.

Chapter Sixteen
Hand in Cap

Two days after Thanksgiving, 1969, Grandmother came to the rescue. She drove up from Arkansas and moved in with Mother. She'd lost her husband of 55 years scarcely two and a half years earlier. But she was as feisty and nearly as energetic as ever. At the age of 77, she was still writing for the hometown newspaper, *The Osceola Times*, still serving on the County Welfare Board and the Women's Missionary Union Board, and still teaching the adult Sunday School class at the Baptist Church.

"A most remarkable lady," her newspaper put it in announcing her move to Nashville. "As a friend to one and all, Mrs. Mae C. Jones is a legend in her own time. Now 77 years old, Mrs. Jones has never decreased the energy and intelligent activity of her mind and body as she has continued to work a full 40-hour week as Society Editor and news writer of the *Times*."

An earlier profile of Grandmother, written five years earlier by her long-time colleague, Phil Mullen, when she was 72, noted that "she works a full eight-hour day at the *Times*—and she works searching out the facts for the continuing stream of friendly, praising news stories which she writes about the people she loves. On the telephone calling some news source, she can say, 'This is Mrs. Jones,' with all the authority of James Reston or Arthur Krock calling some congressman for information for an article in *The New York Times*."

Now it was time for Grandmother to help Mother again. I imagine they had fun together, swapping stories at the dinner table, giggling like schoolgirls through the bath and as Grandmother helped Mother dress for work. Mother even allowed Grandmother to help in the kitchen. That was a good thing, she said, "because I have to use wooden handled utensils, and they're very hard to find. Mine are about chewed up now."

But while Mother couldn't change the sheets, she insisted on making her own bed. "She takes the corners of the sheet in her mouth and pulls them up," Grandmother told Ellington. "Every day before I can get in there, she has her bed made up."

It was like old times. Only it wasn't. For while they each had suffered loss, both were bathed in blessings. Twenty-three years after Mae Canady Jones gave her sweet daughter to a strange young man in marriage, she got to see her shine again.

In Nashville, Grandmother jumped into volunteer work at our church and as a guide at Cheekwood, Nashville's botanical garden. She also enrolled in a series of history classes. That woman never stopped learning. Even Mother had a hard time keeping up with her.

In mid-January 1970, the Nashville chapter of Pilot Club International, a civic service club for professional and executive businesswomen, nominated Mother as "Handicapped Professional Woman of the Year" in a national contest co-sponsored by the President's Committee on Employment of the Handicapped.

President Dwight D. Eisenhower had established the independent federal agency, today called the President's Committee on Employment of People with Disabilities, in 1954. This was the first year it had teamed up with Pilot Club International to recognize "outstanding professional women" with disabilities.

Mother completed the first draft of her application for the award in longhand. That meant she laboriously accomplished the swoops and swirls of handwriting with a pen gripped between her teeth. She wrote the following answer, in the third person, to the question, "How has the nominee helped to further the rehabilitation and employment of other handicapped persons?"

"During World War II," Mother wrote, "she frequently visited Army Hospitals at invitation of the PR officer. The Universal newsreel of her graduation from dental school was shown in many war zones, resulting in extensive correspondence to amputees. Three years were spent as an experimental amputee at UCLA. Presently she participates in training courses for 'Outlook Nashville' and is a frequent speaker at Goodwill Industries and to other rehabilitation groups."

In answer to the question, how will her selection as "Handicapped American of the Year" help other people with handicaps, Mother recalled that she did not receive state support to return to dental school in 1941 because "training an armless dentist could not be justified." For the same reason, her application to the School of Public Health at the University of Michigan was initially rejected because the dean didn't think she'd be able to do the work. Her experience, she wrote, "focuses attention on the fact that creative thinking in the area of training the handicapped is a must. It is to be hoped (that), by selecting the nominee, attention would be called to the many heretofore closed areas. It is to be hoped that other handicapped persons would be inspired to set their goals high."

It was Dad who had introduced Mother to Outlook Nashville through his acquaintance with Jacqueline Page, the organization's program director.

Jackie was born with a rare condition that left her unable to use her arms or legs. Her mother, however, "wouldn't allow me to use the word 'can't,'" Jackie said. Homeschooled through high school, she started attending college courses with the encouragement of Outlook Nashville cofounders Elsa and Henry Ellis, eventually earning her bachelor's and master's degrees and doctorate in human development and counseling from the George Peabody College for Teachers. At Jackie's invitation, Mother joined in the Outlook Nashville training programs and started giving talks to other organizations. Jackie would go on to head the Office for Handicapped Persons for the Metropolitan Government of Nashville and Davidson County.

I've often wondered why people like Mother and Jackie were called "handicapped" in the 1960s and '70s, while today the term is "disability."

"Handicap" was a horse racing term originally derived from the medieval game "Hand in Cap." In the early 1900s, the umpire would put stones on a fast horse to "handicap" it, or slow it down, so the other horses had a chance to win the race. In the competitive, social evolutionist worldview that was prevalent at the time, people with a limp or missing an arm carried burdens, or handicaps, that made it difficult for them to compete in the "race" of life. A handicapped person thus is one who is helpless, hopeless, and who, cap in hand, sits on the corner and begs.

"Disability," on the other hand, refers to a difficulty or "impairment" that hinders one's full participation in society. On the surface, there doesn't seem to be much difference between "handicap" and "disability." But it's all in the way the word is used. It's important not to refer to a person as "disabled;" rather, he or she has a disability, a limitation that only becomes apparent against the restrictions and expectations imposed by an "able" society—steps instead of ramps; cars that require hands to drive; jobs that exclude anyone who is different from the rest.

This was Mother's calling. She refused to be defined by her limitations. In fact, she spent a lifetime struggling to overcome them. In the process, she confounded the expectations of society. Time and again she broke barriers. But not in a haughty or vengeful way. Whenever Mother reached another mountaintop, she humbly praised God. She saw it as her purpose in life to give hope to others. That is why she was such an inspiration. That is why people loved her.

In the spring of 1970, Mother found out she'd been chosen from 17 finalists to be the nation's first "Handicapped Professional Woman of the Year." She was honored on July 19 during the opening dinner of the 49th annual convention of Pilot Club International at the Americana Hotel in Miami Beach. More than 1,000 Pilot Club members from across the United States, Canada, England, France, and Japan attended the six-day meeting. In addition to a plaque and engraved silver bowl, Mother received an invitation to attend the annual meeting of the President's Committee on Employment of the Handicapped in Washington, D.C., in April. For her participation in that meeting, Mother later would receive a Citation for Meritorious Service.

Bob and I couldn't attend the Pilot Club Convention to cheer Mother on. But our grandmother was there, seated at one of the tables at the front of the huge assembly hall, smiling broadly with tears streaming down her cheeks.

Later, Dr. William H. Allen, dean of the Meharry School of Dentistry, sang her praises in an article published that fall in the American Dental Association *News*. "She is a most pleasant person to work with," he said, "and if you did not know visually that she was an armless person, you would never be aware of it judging from her work or accomplishments."

What Mother said in receiving her award shall remain a mystery; she apparently did not save a copy of her acceptance speech. A newspaper account records only a single statement: "I never felt I was handicapped—merely inconvenienced." However, among Mother's papers is a handwritten series of notes on a piece of lined yellow notebook paper that could have been a first, rough outline of her speech. The outline includes three quotations about gratitude, including this one by the early 20th century American poet Edwin Arlington Robinson:

> *"... for every gift*
> *"Or sacrifice, there are—or there may be—*
> *"Two kinds of gratitude: the sudden kind*
> *"We feel for what we take, the larger kind*
> *"We feel for what we give."*

That spring, I finished my bachelor's degree, cum laude, in American Studies at Amherst. I'd chosen a topic that, through my parents' experiences, I knew well: "Black Colleges: The Struggle for Life and Values." In my conclusion, I wrote: "Black colleges, by heroically struggling to provide an education for disadvantaged black students and by orienting themselves in the direction of the deprived areas of society, are setting a moral example for the rest of the nation."

It's rather amazing to think, as I look back at it now, that both of my parents ended up working for historically Black institutions. Don't get me wrong: my parents were not high-nosed missionaries who swooped in to give aid and comfort to those less fortunate than themselves. I don't believe Mother and Dad had a racist bone in their bodies. The pigment of one's skin did not have any particular significance to them. They saw people as people; that was that.

But I believe this was a path Mother had been walking since she was a young girl. Playing with the farmhands' children on the plantation; visiting segregated schools in Flint, Michigan, to talk about health and disease prevention; and, ultimately, becoming one of a very few white professors in a college that even today turns out roughly 20% of the nation's Black doctors and dentists.

"I felt I had an opportunity there to try to show the best qualities of a white person that I could," she told an interviewer in 1997. "And have a good relationship with the Black people. From the maids and janitors on up."

This had been an intentional walk for Mother. I don't mean that she had the foresight to find these opportunities. No. But it was more than chance. Mother believed a Higher Power was guiding her feet. As Grandmother had insisted after her daughter lost her arms, God had a plan for Margaret Jones Chanin. Perhaps Mother's purpose was to teach. Perhaps it was, simply and profoundly, to touch the lives of others.

What was Dad's purpose? Was it taking the job at Tennessee State? I doubt he thought of it that way. Dad bounced through life like a billiard ball, from side rail to corner pocket and back again. There didn't seem to be any intention or direction to his moves. He usually took the first job he could get.

On the other hand, Dad's propensity to complain about injustices and flaws he perceived in "the system," as well as people, probably helped those who were trying to stop the state from expanding the Nashville campus of the University of Tennessee. Their lawsuit, filed in 1968, alleged that TSU had been systematically deprived of funds over many decades, hampering its efforts to educate and enable Blacks to attain their fair share of the American dream. Perhaps this was God's plan for Dad's life—he was the pebble that triggers an avalanche, the anonymous soul who sets off a chain of events that ultimately overturns an oppressive social order. Dad was a bit player. His performance was brief. Within six years of arriving in Nashville, he left academia forever.

Surely, I was thinking about Mother's heroic struggles and her impressive achievements at Meharry when I chose the title for my thesis. Dad had struggled, too, but in the end, he gave up the good fight. Why? To try to answer that question, I would have to meet my father where he was now—on the other side of the world.

Upon arrival in Israel in January 1970, Dad lived in an "absorption center" for new immigrants in Tel Aviv, where he studied Hebrew and attended a course for the "reorientation of graduated chemists for the oil industry." Within a few months, he'd landed a job in Dimona, about 20 miles west of the Dead Sea in the Negev desert, near Beersheba, mixing chemicals for clothing dyes. He worked for a big textile factory where the bales of cotton come in one end and clothes come out the other.

I visited him during the summer of 1970, after I graduated from Amherst. I was in England that summer for a social work program, and I lived with an English couple in the village of Keynsham, near Bristol. Afterwards, I took the "Orient Express," the classic, 1,700-mile train ride from London to Istanbul made famous by the novelist Agatha Christie. In those days, a ticket for the four-day route through Belgium, Germany, Austria, Yugoslavia, and Bulgaria cost 60 British pounds, about $44. From Istanbul, I caught a plane to Tel Aviv.

During our time together, Dad seemed happy. I hadn't seen him so relaxed in years. Part of it was the slower pace, I'm sure, and the absence of the push-and-shove tension that always seems to be a part of academic life. I was happier and more relaxed, too, so that also made it easier for us to get along. But I think a major contributor to his genial temperament was his feeling that he was contributing in some significant way to this new nation that had been carved out of the desert to save the Jewish people.

Although he never really learned Hebrew, Dad spoke German, and because there were so many scientists who'd emigrated from Germany during and after World War II, he could communicate with his colleagues at work. But his old pattern of not being able to hold a position for very long repeated itself, even in Israel. Following my visit, Dad continued to bounce from job to job, and from city to city. Within a few months, he moved to the ancient port city of Haifa, where he got a job as a chemist with a pharmaceutical firm. In Haifa, he also met and moved in with a divorced woman named Ellen and her teenage son, Ari.

After my return to Amherst in the fall of 1970, and supported by a fellowship, I began a one-year term as Amherst's sports information director.

I wrote the copy for the football program, ran the press box at football games, and supervised the undergraduate sports news service. I also started taking classes in the School of Education on the Amherst campus of the University of Massachusetts, working toward my master's degree in Higher Education.

In January 1971, I accepted a position as a Head of Residence at UMass Amherst. I was responsible for 200 undergraduate women who lived on the first eight floors of a 22-story dormitory. The other Heads of Residence at the university were planning careers in Higher Education as deans and administrators. After completing my master's degree in January 1972, I continued my studies toward a doctorate in the School of Education.

That spring, I took three courses in the Human Relations area of the School of Education. The other graduate students I met in these classes were planning to become psychotherapists. Over the course of that semester, I realized I had much more in common with them than with my fellow Heads of Residence. So, I decided to become a psychologist and psychotherapist. Essentially, I chose a career by choosing a peer group!

Philip after graduating from Amherst

Chapter Seventeen
An Answered Prayer

In June 1972, Mother learned that she and six other Meharry faculty members had been selected as Outstanding Educators of America for their professional and civic achievements. Five of the seven, including her boss, Dr. Eugenia Mobley, were from the School of Dentistry. Based in Chicago, *Outstanding Educators of America* was an annual awards program and publication honoring distinguished men and women for their exceptional service, achievements, and leadership in higher education.

The next year, in 1973, Mother was promoted to Director of the Oral Disease Control Clinic at Meharry. By now she had an electric typewriter, which enabled her to compose a letter quite rapidly, with a stick clenched between her teeth.

"Cancers of the mouth afflict some 23,000 Americans annually and kill about 8,000," she noted in a letter to a state official. "So many deaths arising from a site so easily observed underline the need for a more intensive program of education. The need to have oral screening programs is a direct result of less than 40% of the population seeing a dentist on a preventive basis (regular checkup); therefore, a high percentage of cancers are diagnosed too late, when pain has demanded attention."

Meharry's Early Oral Cancer Detection Program, she continued, focused on a target population of those over 35 who smoked and/or used alcohol. "We found the most efficient method was to go directly to the plant or office, usually in a First Aid area where a sink and an outlet for a headlight were available. A straight chair with a portable headrest is adequate for the examination. One dentist and one assistant could screen approximately 20-25 (people) per hour."

That fall, Dad was in the middle of a war zone.

In 1973, the Day of Atonement, the holiest of Jewish holy days, fell on October 6. On that day, Syrian and Egyptian armies launched a surprise attack against Israeli Defense Forces to regain territory lost during the Six-Day War of 1967. The fighting was furious. Within 16 days, the Israelis repelled both the Syrians and Egyptians, and a ceasefire was brokered by the United Nations.

Dad didn't talk about the war much, but among his papers is Ellen's five-page typewritten personal account of life in Haifa during the conflict. For several days, while the city imposed a blackout and suspended bus service, "Martin spent his evenings doing the family laundry," she wrote. "He also baked uncounted sweet cakes, until the egg shortage hit. These cakes I delivered every day. I think that we have the only army that had homemade cakes and fresh fruit every day."

Late that year, Mother received a legal document from Israel. Written in Hebrew on thin parchment paper and accompanied by an English translation, the document from the County Religious Court in Haifa noted that Martin Chanin, an Israeli citizen, had asked the court in October to end his civil marriage to a U.S. citizen so he could marry again in "the law of Moses and Israel." The court, in its ruling of divorce dated November 22, agreed.

I can't remember if Mother shared the divorce decree with me at the time. I was immersed in my work and studies. I can only imagine that with Grandmother's unfailing love and support, Mother carried on, as she always had. In fact, her 1973 Christmas letter was one of the most cheerful ones she'd ever written.

"Dear Friends," she began, "isn't it wonderful that God has provided each of us with so much to do that time need never drag? My wandering son,

Bob, is still in England, where he spent last winter and summer in Devon and Cornwall, building barns and packing mackerel. He is now in London saving for the next trip; present plans include India and points East. Phil spent 10 days with Bob in June in England, as he traveled to Athens to spend a wonderful month with Ottie and Charles Arrington (*our former pastor in Clemson*) ... I am still teaching in the dental school at Meharry Medical College. The challenge of playing a small part in helping students to develop a philosophy of preventive dentistry keeps each day exciting."

I have no idea why Dad divorced Mother. He never remarried, and he never really left her, at least not emotionally. In Haifa, he struggled to get along with Ellen's son—another old pattern. Within a year or two, he'd moved on to Tiberius, on the western shore of the Sea of Galilee. There he found a job in a laboratory as an analytical and food chemist for kibbutzim (agricultural collectives). He worked at a center that converted farm products into fish and animal food. He provided quality control—ensuring the product had proper amounts of proteins, fats, and carbohydrates. I visited him there during the summer of 1976. While in Tiberius, Dad saw a woman limping down the street and approached her. Her leg had been maimed in an accident. They developed a relationship and eventually moved in together.

Dad had found someone else to take care of.

The accolades for Mother kept coming. In April 1975, the National Women Executives honored her with their "Lady Executive of the Year" during their Sixth Annual Awards Dinner at the Brentwood Country Club, just south of Nashville in Williamson County. Country music star Brenda Lee received the Community Service Award, and Oprah Winfrey, a local TV newscaster, who would go on to become an international celebrity in her own right, received an Executive Award.

The next month, Mother's work at the Meharry School of Dentistry was showcased during Huell Howser's Happy Features segment on WSM-TV. Howser, a native of Gallatin, just north of Nashville, produced the series of documentaries about people with handicaps who were making significant contributions to their communities.

My doctoral dissertation that spring, entitled "A Comprehensive Case Study in the Training of Residential Hall Assistants," described an educational process for improving interpersonal skills and competencies of those responsible for the safety and guidance of undergraduate students. But even before I'd earned my doctorate, my heart led me to take a deeper look at the human relationships that shaped my interior life and the way I perceived the world.

During graduate school in 1974, I helped start a men's group. When I shared with the group about my unsatisfying experiences with transcendental meditation, one of the men urged me to attend the Naropa Institute in Boulder, Colorado, to experience a more authentic Buddhist meditation. That I did.

Asian immigrants had introduced Buddhism into the United States in the 19th century, although not so much in the South. In the mid-1950s, "Beat Generation" poets and writers including Gary Snyder, Jack Kerouac and Allen Ginsberg embraced Zen as part of their exploration of sexual liberation, psychedelic drugs, and a decidedly anti-materialistic, bohemian lifestyle. A decade later Joseph Goldstein and Jack Kornfield encountered Buddhism while volunteering for the Peace Corps in India and in Thailand as an alternative to serving in Vietnam. Upon their return to the States, Goldstein and Kornberg joined Sharon Salzberg, who had studied Buddhist meditation practices in India, and began teaching Vipassana meditation and mindfulness practices at the Naropa Institute, a center of "contemplative education" founded in 1974 by Tibetan Buddhist abbot, meditation master, and scholar Chogyam Trungpa Rinpoche.

The next summer, after finishing my doctorate at UMass, I enrolled in an intensive five-week course in Vipassana meditation at Naropa. Vipassana, roughly translated as '"insight"' meditation, is the oldest Buddhist meditation practice, a set of exercises dedicated to making the practitioner more aware of his or her mental life. Under the guidance of our teachers, my fellow pupils and I meditated three to four hours a day, and all day on Sundays. We studied the writings of mystical practitioners of many faiths, including the contemporary Trappist monk Thomas Merton, the Sufis, the Hasidic masters, the desert monks of Palestine and of course, the Buddhist texts. While these mystics represented diverse perspectives, stretching across continents and over 2,000 years, I marveled at how similar their conclusions were about the nature of God and spiritual practice.

That summer's experience at Naropa gave me a perspective that has strongly shaped my path, has stayed with me, and has led me to continue to read, to meditate, and to look for the intersections of spiritual and psychotherapy practice. The writings of Jack Kornfield, a clinical psychologist who trained as a Buddhist monk, have been particularly influential, not only to me but also to a few of my clients with whom I have shared them. How interesting it is that my professional work and my spiritual path seem to use the same compass!

Upon returning to Amherst in the fall of 1975, I took post-doctoral training in clinical psychology, even as I was determined to continue my "awakening within."

Not so my father. He continued to miss significant events in his family's life. Dad did not attend the funerals of either of his parents, not his mother's service in 1970 or his father's service in early 1976. Nor did he attend Bob's wedding that spring.

On the previous Labor Day weekend, in 1975, Bob had met a lovely and devout young woman while undertaking religious studies in North Carolina. A graduate of the University of North Carolina at Chapel Hill, Cindy worked for the Campus Crusade for Christ. Bob fell madly in love, and they married in May 1976.

In early February 1977, Bob and Cindy were attending an evangelical institute in North Carolina when Bob received an urgent phone call from Mother.

"Your grandmother has died," she said. "Please come home. I need you."

Grandmother died on February 5, 1977. She was 84 years old.

"Osceola has lost one of her great ladies," the obituary in her hometown newspaper began. After recalling her impressive career as a journalist, the article concluded with lines from one of her favorite poems, "Ulysses," by the English poet laureate Alfred, Lord Tennyson:

I am a part of all that I have met
Yet all experience is an arch wherethro'
Gleams that untravell'd world whose margin fades
For ever and forever when I move.
How dull it is to pause, to make an end,
To rust unburnish'd, not to shine in use!

Grandmother certainly did shine. Though born a country girl, she was a lover of education and had an inquisitive mind. She passed that passion onto her grandchildren, including Aunt Louise's daughter, Margo Thorning, who grew up to become a Ph.D.-level economist. "She got this from you," Louise told Mae at some point. When Margo was a little girl, Louise recalled, "she would ask you a question, and you would say, 'Well, let's look it up.'"

Grandmother was the most loyal and nurturing person—besides Mother—I've ever met. And she was fearless. She marched for the vote for women. In 1933, she put her 16-year-old daughter on the train to Chicago—by herself—so she could finish high school. And when, after the accident, her disfigured daughter prayed for death, Grandmother responded, "Absolutely not!" She always said "no" to darkness, limitation, and denial, and "yes" to openness, freedom, and living life to the fullest.

Grandmother was buried next to Granddad in Pleasant Hill Cemetery in Brunswick, Tennessee. Bob and I served as pallbearers. Afterwards, I returned to Amherst, where I was working as a residence hall director at UMass. Later that year, I interned in a nearby mental health center. Bob and Cindy went back to the church institute in South Carolina, while Mother went home to an empty house.

That must have been incredibly hard. Grandmother had been a fount of steadiness and strength for 36 years, ever since the accident. She was always there to remind Mother that there was a purpose and meaning to her life, to urge her to find that purpose and rise to her highest potential. And, for the last seven years, she had been Mother's constant and most intimate companion and friend.

What was Mother going to do now? Go to work, of course.

After all, it wasn't like she'd never experienced loss before. When darkness was all around her, Mother leaned on her faith. She always looked for the light and the good. She was always open to new opportunities to help others, and to allow others to help her.

One evening when she got home from work, Mother walked two doors down to ask her neighbor, Betty Weitemeyer, if she would help her unbutton her jacket. We'd known the Weitemeyers since we moved to the Richland-West End neighborhood in 1963. Betty was a bright spot in our neighborhood.

But on this night, she was not herself. Mother apologized for her unexpected arrival. As Betty helped her out of her jacket, Mother asked, "Are you okay?"

Betty sighed, "I've been sitting here holding my hands all day wondering why I quit my job. My doctor said it was too much for me, standing on my feet all day. But now what do I do?"

For Betty had always worked. Born in Scotland in 1916, she'd immigrated with her family to the United States during the Great Depression. They settled in Chicago, where her father got a job on the railroad. Betty wanted to be a missionary when she grew up. But then she met George Weitemeyer, the son of German immigrants. George was a printer who worked for the Rand McNally map and atlas company. Five children later, in 1959, George was transferred to Nashville, where his company had opened a ticket-printing division. That's where Betty's dream of helping other people came true, only in a way she'd never visualized.

By the early 1960s, women were entering the workforce as never before. Many had young children. But this was before the advent of childcare centers. If there were no family members nearby willing and able to take care of the children during the day, how were the mothers ever going to hold down a job? Betty filled the gap. She opened her home to the children of others. Not only that, but Betty was also a fine cook and baker. When her own children had left the nest, she took a job as kitchen supervisor at East Nashville Junior High. But all that standing had taken a toll on her legs.

"I shouldn't complain," Betty said. "Especially to you."

Mother nodded. "Since Marty left, it's been hard finding someone to help me get dressed in the morning."

Betty cocked her head to one side as if a glimpse of the future had just been revealed to her. "Wait a minute," she said. "I've been feeling sorry for myself because I'm retired and suddenly have all this time on my hands. I know what I can do. I can help you. Margaret, please, I'll help you anyway I can."

And that's how Betty became Mother's constant and always-cheerful caregiver. For the next 11 years, every morning Betty came to the house to bathe and dress her. Every evening, Mother ate dinner with Betty and her husband George. After dinner, Betty would walk two doors down to Mother's house to help her into her nightclothes and tuck her in for the night. Years later, Mother recalled, "I couldn't have dreamed of anybody that could have been this caring."

Another answered prayer—for them both.

In early 1977 Mother received a phone call from an old friend, Bruce Richards. The sailboat-loving little boy from Florence, Alabama, was all grown up now. He was applying to medical school at Vanderbilt, and he wondered if he could stay with her the night before his interview. He didn't have a car and Mother lived just a few blocks from campus—an easy walk. "Of course!" Mother replied. It would be good to have a young man stay in the house again.

That night, instead of dining at the Weitemeyers, Mother made dinner for two. Bruce fed Mother and they talked and talked. Bruce had "aced" the Medical College Admissions Test and was meeting the next morning with Dr. John Exton, a member of the medical school's admission committee.

Exton, who like Bruce's parents was from New Zealand, was one of two reasons Bruce wanted to come to Vanderbilt. The other was the Appalachian Student Health Coalition, which had been established in 1969 by a Vanderbilt medical student, Bill Dow, to bring health care to remote communities in the mountains of East Tennessee. Aided by the former chairman of Pediatrics at Vanderbilt, Dr. Amos Christie, and by Dr. Leslie Falk, a Rhodes scholar and civil rights advocate who chaired the Department of Family and Community Medicine at Meharry, the effort was supported by a grant from a prominent health care philanthropy, the Josiah Macy Jr. Foundation. By the late 1970s, the coalition was holding health fairs in small towns throughout the region.

"That was the hook for me," Bruce said. "This whole notion that we are here to serve was part of the Chanin household and part of mine. That's what we're here for."

That spring, Mother was invited by President Jimmy Carter to participate in a White House Conference on Handicapped Individuals in Washington, D.C.

Congress had passed a law prohibiting discrimination against people with handicaps in 1973. But Joseph Califano, Carter's secretary of Health, Education and Welfare, didn't sign regulations implementing the law until April 1976, after picketers showed up at HEW offices around the country and even at his home. The regulations, which required all institutions receiving HEW funds to remove barriers to people with handicaps, were not uncontested. Critics complained about the millions of dollars it would cost to install wheelchair ramps and larger bathroom stalls in public buildings, and wheelchair lifts on public buses.

To Mother, the regulations were a matter of fairness that should be extended to tax policy as well. When her children were small, she had to hire someone to help care for them, but she couldn't claim the woman's salary as a deduction, only the time she provided actual nursing care. People with disabilities may make good salaries, but by the time they pay for attendant care and specialized housing, "they are reduced to the poverty level," she told a reporter at the conclusion of the conference. "We think that ought to be deducted as a necessary business expense."

Mother was one of 15 delegates from Tennessee, and 700 nationwide, who attended the conference, which opened on May 23, 1977, with an address by President Carter. "For too long, handicapped people have been deprived of a right to an education," Carter began. "For too long, handicapped people have been excluded from the possibility of jobs and employment where they could support themselves. For too long, handicapped people have been kept out of buildings, have been kept off streets and sidewalks, have been excluded from private and public transportation, and have been deprived of a simple right in many instances just to communicate with one another.

"You're intelligent, courageous leaders," the president told the delegates. "But because you have experienced suffering and because you have overcome it, I think the recommendations that will be coming from you that will affect the lives of many millions of people now and in the future will have that same extra dimension. Our country needs you, and I know that you will never disappoint those who look to you for leadership."

The conference was organized into a series of state caucuses and concurrent workshops, within which the delegates deliberated on several thousand recommendations for "equalizing opportunities" for Americans with disabilities. The rigid scheduling and voluminous agenda left some delegates feeling angry and disillusioned. "The failure of this conference is we got no opportunity to say anything clearly on any issue," Adrienne Asch, a conference observer who worked for the New York State Division of Human Rights, told the *New York Times*.

Mother came away with a different impression. "We ended on a very positive note," she told *The Tennessean*, adding that she felt the delegates "had gotten the ear of the various powers-that-be in Washington."

Besides, she got to meet the Rev. Harold Wilke. A delegate from New York, the United Church of Christ minister was already nationally known for his social activism. Born without arms on a Missouri farm in 1914, he fought against all forms of discrimination his entire life. A social activist who was arrested in the civil rights marches in the 1960s, Wilke was one of the first Americans with a severe disability to serve as a parish minister.

After World War II, he began to counsel disabled veterans and their families. He wrote four books on coping with disabilities in daily life, including *Using Everything You've Got*, published in 1976. Upon Wilke's death in 2003, his son John told *The Los Angeles Times* that his father taught himself to drive with his left foot on the steering wheel, and in 1968 drove his family all the way across the country that way.

"He obviously couldn't shake hands with people," added Alan Reich, then-president of the National Organization on Disability, "but he would put his head against another person's head – embrace without hugging."

Sounds like Mother, doesn't he?

Chapter Eighteen
How to Survive a Bear Attack

On August 13, 1977, Cynthia Dusel-Bacon, a 30-year-old geologist from California, was dropped off by helicopter—alone—on a ridge about 60 miles southeast of Fairbanks to map the geology of the region for the Alaskan Geology Branch of the U.S. Geological Survey. Mapping is a key component in the evaluation of potential mineral resources.

This was not Cynthia's first solo mapping field season. She had worked in the remote area the previous two summers. And she was well trained. Careful not to startle and instead to forewarn any bears that might be in the vicinity, she always made plenty of noise, such as calling out as she walked, and hammering on rocks with her geologist's hammer as she collected samples.

But this summer would be different.

After walking down along a game trail that led through tangles of birch brush and over rough, rocky slopes, Cynthia had stopped at a large outcrop of rock to break off a sample when she heard a large crash. A black bear rose from the undergrowth, just 10 feet below her. Cynthia started yelling and banging on rocks with her hammer. Undeterred, the female bear moved up the slope and circled the geologist, then knocked her flat on her face from behind. Cynthia had no way to defend herself. She did not carry a gun, and the rock hammer flew out of her hand when she was struck by 175 pounds of muscle and fur.

"I froze, not instinctively but deliberately, remembering that playing dead was supposed to cause an attacking bear to lose interest and go away," Cynthia recalled in an account she wrote for *Alaska* magazine in 1979. Instead, she said, "I felt the sudden, piercing pain of the bear's teeth biting deep in my shoulder."

Cynthia tried to reach the walkie-talkie radio in the left outside pocket of her backpack with her left arm, but she couldn't release the buckle of the flap that secured the radio. "My movement caused the bear to start a new flurry of biting and tearing at the flesh of my upper right arm," she said. "I was completely conscious of feeling my flesh torn, teeth against bone, but the sensation was more of numb horror at what was happening to me ... After chewing on my right shoulder, arm, and side repeatedly, the bear began to bite my head and tear at my scalp."

Cynthia forced herself to stay calm and focus on her breathing. She had to remain conscious. If she went into shock, there was no chance of survival. Married only five months earlier to fellow geologist Charlie Bacon, she wondered if she'd see her husband again. "What a way to go," she thought.

The bear bit through Cynthia's right shoulder and dragged her down a slope through heavy brush and rocks. After about a half hour, the bear stopped. Panting heavily, she sat down to rest about four feet away from her helpless prey. At this point, Cynthia was able to use her uninjured left arm to pull the radio from its pouch. Stealthily, she snapped on the radio switch, pulled the antenna partially up, and pushed the button to activate the transmitter.

Holding the radio close to her mouth, she called to the helicopter pilot as loudly as she dared, "Ed, this is Cynthia. Come quick. I'm being eaten by a bear!"

She tried to give her location, but seeing her movement, the bear attacked again, knocking the radio out of her hand. "I screamed in pain as I felt my good arm being torn and mangled by claws and teeth," she said.

About 10 minutes later, Cynthia heard the faint sound of a helicopter. It seemed to circle, then flew away. Ed couldn't spot her and had flown back to pick up one of the other geologists on the team to help with the search. Another 10 minutes elapsed, then the helicopter returned. This time she was spotted. The pilot flew low enough to scare off the bear, but he left again to pick up another geologist to aid in the rescue. Fifty agonizing minutes after the attack began, Cynthia was rescued.

Cynthia was flown to the Fort Greeley army base in Delta Junction, about an hour away, where her condition was stabilized, and then to Fort Wainwright Army Hospital in Fairbanks, where her badly mauled left arm was amputated six inches below the shoulder. Doctors grafted a vein from her left thigh under her badly damaged right arm to try to maintain its blood supply before she was flown to Stanford University Hospital near her home in Woodside, south of San Francisco. Ten days later, however, a blood clot formed in the transplanted vessel, and she developed a high fever, suggestive of infection. Doctors had no choice but to amputate the right arm at the shoulder.

Cynthia was discharged from the hospital six weeks later, after new tissue and skin grafts had filled in the hole on her right side. The bear was eventually tracked and killed by the Alaska Fish and Game Department.

In September, Cindy Chanin showed her mother-in-law a newspaper story about the bear attack.

"Oh, the poor child!" Mother gasped. Flashing back to that horrible day in July 1941, when she discovered that she, too, had lost her arms, Mother knew Cynthia Dusel-Bacon's ordeal was just beginning. As was characteristic for my mother, that very night she composed a letter, inviting Cynthia and her husband to visit her in Nashville.

A flurry of correspondence followed: letters dictated by Cynthia to Charlie, and responses typed by Mother, with a pencil gripped between her teeth. Cynthia told Mother how Reverend Wilke, the armless advocate whom Mother had met in May 1977 at the White House Conference on Handicapped Individuals, had come to visit her while she was recovering in the hospital.

"He showed me how he was 100 percent independent and a 100-percent foot user," Cynthia said. "He also connected me with a woman who became my foot mentor. Mary Lisch was born with no arms and did everything with her feet. I took up what she did, which was to put a bar stool on castors in the kitchen. I'd step up onto it, and I'd be at the right height to put my feet in the sink and on the counter."

By curling her toes around a specially retrofitted knife, Cynthia can cut up vegetables. She can push cans into the electric can opener and perform countless household tasks with her feet that previously required the use of her arms. Still, she wondered. How do they DO it? How do people make a new life for themselves after they have lost their arms? In February 1978, she and Charlie accepted Mother's invitation and flew to Nashville to find out.

She discovered that her and Mother's amputations were "mirror images" of each other—one at the shoulder and one short, above the elbow. Cynthia chose to use bilateral prostheses, while Mother relied on a single, right arm prosthesis. Yet Cynthia soon realized that this "inconvenience," as Mother often referred to her situation, did not impair her ability to live a full and fulfilling life.

"She took us to the Grand Ole Opry, which was wonderful because both my husband and I are big country music fans," Cynthia recalled in 2021. "We went with her grocery shopping, and I remember specifically seeing how she would not push the cart, but rather stick her hook into the mesh in the side of the cart and pull the cart. I thought, 'Oh, yeah! That makes a lot of sense.'

"I remember going to a party with her. It was a daytime event, and as soon as we got there, she went into the bedroom of the hostess who was a good friend of hers, and she said, 'I want to take my arm off to be at the party.' And I thought, 'Gee, that's funny. You'd think you'd just want to keep it on.' Well, now I always try to take mine off when I'm at somebody's house where I'm comfortable. If I'm not using them, I prefer to not to be wearing them. I'll put on a poncho. That was the first time I realized that maybe artificial arms aren't everything they're cracked up to be, because they're heavy and can be uncomfortable.

"A lot of the time we just talked," Cynthia continued. "One of the major things I got from her was just psychologically to see a woman who could continue a scientific career by modifying what she did. She was a role model for an independent, accomplished, but physically limited, professional woman. She was able to maintain her prestige and accomplishments, and just move over to teach what she knew, even though she couldn't do it. She was very supportive and gave me great hope.

"Coming home from that I was quite buoyed in my morale. There are many ways to continue in a profession. She taught dentistry. For me, the corollary is that I could plan all my Alaskan fieldwork, which one has to do to be a geologist, and then direct my husband to be the executor of the sample collecting, since I can't swing a hammer. He's also in charge of carrying a gun for protection from bears! There are so many different aspects to geology. Some of it's computer-based, and a big part is writing papers about your research and making geologic maps. You can always get around the physical obstacles if you have support. For me that support was my husband.

"The U.S. Geological Survey was also super supportive. My branch chief saw to it that my petrographic microscope, used to examine thin sections (slices) of rocks, was modified to have foot controls and levers on the instrument. Describing the mineralogy and textures in thin sections was the first thing I was able to do after my accident that showed I could still contribute to the field of geology."

Charlie Bacon and Cynthia Dusel-Bacon in the Alaska Range conducting geologic fieldwork, 2005

Mother encouraged Cynthia to get help when she needed it, and to let nothing get in the way of living a normal life. When Charlie was out doing fieldwork during the summers, Cynthia asked neighbors or her mother-in-law, who lived nearby, for help. "I was able to stay by myself, which meant a lot," she said. After their son, Ian, was born in 1986, "and my husband would go off to the field, I'd have someone stay with me and our son. Then once he was maybe 6, he could help me do things."

Cynthia went on to have a 39-year career with the U.S. Geological Survey. Now retired, she is Scientist Emerita in the Survey's Geology, Minerals, Energy, and Geophysics Science Center in Menlo Park, California. Her son is married and living in Pittsburgh, and she and Charlie, also retired, continue to enjoy a "very rich life" together.

It did take a while, she admitted, to get used to people staring at her when she was out in public. Once while banking, Cynthia was startled by the piercing voice of a young child yelling, "Mommy, Mommy, that lady has monster arms!" Now she can smile at a child's innocent outburst.

Before Cynthia lost her arms, when she saw a person with a disability, she might have thought, "Oh, what a poor person with such a limited life." Now, thanks in part to Mother's influence and her own experiences, "I always think they must have overcome many challenges," she said, "and have a fascinating life story."

Even after we left home, Bob and I continued the special relationship we'd developed growing up. Our strongest bond was forged through basketball. Bob and I both played basketball in high school and, later, in college. I would come home from college for vacation and in the summers, and we would always be looking for a basketball court to play on. Depending upon the vacation, we'd call our games the Thanksgiving Bowl or the Christmas Bowl. If it were too cold to play outside, we'd sneak into a local gym. If it were closed and locked up for the holidays, we'd pry open a window and crawl inside. Often, we'd play one-on-one, sometimes for hours. If we could find two other players, we'd play as a team—Bob and me. We rarely lost. We'd played together so much that we always knew where the other would be on the court, and we could pass off to each other without even having to look.

Following high school and college, Bob had many adventures. While I was in Massachusetts, he moved in with me for a time and got a job in a metal plating factory. Once, when he had a seizure, he narrowly avoided falling into a vat of molten metal. He hitchhiked through Mexico and spent several months living on the beach with friends 150 miles up the Pacific coast from Acapulco. Then he moved to the westernmost tip of England, where he packed mackerel on the docks of Penzance.

In early 1978, however, Bob struggled to find his way. He'd dropped out of college and had hoped to enter the ministry but when that didn't work out, he started drinking heavily. "I was pregnant about that time," Cindy recalls. "We'd been married almost two years. I went to North Carolina to visit my family and Bob left me a note … He came back after a month."

For a time, Cindy found work as resident manager at the Deer Lake Retirement Community, just south of downtown Nashville, and the family moved into a unit there. "But Bob still didn't have a regular job," she said, and so after Christopher was born in September, they moved in with Mother.

That's about the time that Bruce Richards began his studies at Vanderbilt Medical School. Beginning in the fall of 1978 and for the next four years, "every Saturday night I'd go over to Margaret's. I'd do my laundry and cook her dinner," he said. "I'd usually make a quiche, feed her and just listen." They'd talk about life, and love, and then Betty would come over and get her ready for bed. "Margaret had a remarkable way of navigating life and relationships," Bruce observed.

Cindy agreed. While she felt that Mother tended to compensate for Bob's shortcomings, her mother-in-law took pains not to insert herself into the couple's affairs. "She was very generous," Cindy said. "She had a pattern of helping people."

Eventually, Bob and Cindy found a new church family in Gallatin, a half hour north of Nashville, and they bought a house there. But Bob still struggled, bouncing from job to job. His drinking and drug use eventually got worse and led to run-ins with the law. He cycled through five different treatment programs and spent a month in jail before finally achieving lasting sobriety.

"These were heartbreaks for Margaret," Bruce observed, "but she soldiered through, and tried to keep hope alive that things would get better."

After medical school, Bruce moved to Birmingham for his residency at the University of Alabama. In 1985, he and his wife Sherrie, also a physician, returned to Nashville, where he joined a medical group. He remained one of Mother's closest friends.

In 1979, I moved to Narberth, a borough eight miles northwest of Philadelphia on the historic Pennsylvania Railroad's Main Line. I completed postdoctoral training at the Devereux Foundation in Philadelphia, a non-profit organization that serves children and adults with developmental, emotional and behavioral disorders, and mental illnesses, and I opened a private practice in clinical psychology in Ardmore, just up the line from Narberth.

That summer, I visited Dad in Israel. By then he was back in Tel Aviv, where he had basically stopped working. He referred to himself as self-employed, and had moved in with Paula, the woman with the injured leg he'd met in Tiberius.

Throughout his years in Israel, Dad and I corresponded frequently by mail. I'd send him "CARE" packages filled with items he couldn't get in Israel—caulking compound, cologne, tax-free bourbon, even a backscratcher—and he'd offer me unsolicited advice about my life.

But lately, Dad's letters had become increasingly critical and demanding. In October 1979, he berated me for not thanking him promptly for hosting me that summer. "A thank you note for a visit should be written <u>immediately</u>," he wrote, underlining his irritation. "Your thank you letter was written over two weeks after you returned. This is <u>inexcusable</u>."

Despite this mistreatment, I continued to engage with my father. I was following my script as a good, codependent son.

In June 1979, Mother received a Fellowship Award from the Tennessee Dental Association, its highest honor. The award recognizes Tennessee dentists "who make noteworthy contributions of their time and talent toward professional progress and the public they serve." Eleven dentists were honored; she was the only woman. The awards were presented during the association's annual meeting at the Opryland Hotel in Nashville. More than 1,000 dentists attended.

Prior to the meeting, Mother was interviewed by Elise David, a reporter for the *Nashville Banner*, the city's evening newspaper. The feature, entitled "Dentistry Teacher Lost Her Arms, But Kept Her Dream," described how "she drives a specially designed car, cooks, writes, puts on makeup, opens doors, carries her supplies, and brushes her teeth. The only thing that really frustrates her is that she has yet to find a can opener she can operate ... She's even had some people stay in her home and see the routine she follows."

Added Mother, "They can see in a few days what it took me 10 years to learn.

"I love dentistry," Mother continued. "I'm not sure some of the other professions would have made a place for me. I don't think of myself as handicapped – more as inconvenienced. I want to forget it, and I'm so glad when others do. Just the other day, a woman here who sells Avon mentioned that she had just received some new nail polish colors. I asked what color she thought I would like."

Friends urged Mother to write a book. "I never spent time keeping a diary," she said. "I was too busy living. God has a plan, and he expects us to use all he's left us. I think I've developed a much deeper appreciation for people than if I'd had arms. When one door closes in your face, another opens."

"My life is meaningful, and God helps me focus on the positive," she told another interviewer. "I have had doubts and disappointments, but I have never felt that God did not love me or that He caused the accident. I believe in a God of love. My goal is, in the words of the Apostle Paul, to forget those things which are behind, and reach forth unto those things which are before (Philippians 3:13). I thank God for helping me and using me."

In March 1982, Mother received a letter from her alma mater, the University of Texas Dental Branch at Houston, informing her that the female faculty had created a new scholastic award named for her, and asking if she would present it to the first recipient—Rebecca Maxwell—during the Dental Branch Awards Convocation in May.

The Margaret Jones Chanin Award was created to recognize outstanding female undergraduate students who had achieved excellence in both academic scholarship and clinical practice. "As a female graduate of this school and a pioneer of women in dentistry," the letter continued, "your courage, success and dedication to the profession provide an inspiring image for this special award."

Of course, Mother would attend the convocation, as she would three years later, when the Baylor Alumni Association presented her with a Distinguished Alumnus Award. With characteristic humility, she responded that it was an honor to be recognized in this way.

On May 20, 1982, Mother stood at a podium in front of hundreds of students, faculty and alumni of the school that had rescued her—41 years ago—from the dark hole into which she'd plunged after she lost her arms. Twelve days before her 65th birthday, she remained a picture of health, beauty, and serenity. Tastefully dressed, as always, with not a strand of her impeccably styled hair out of place, she gazed out at her audience, eyes sparkling, her mouth drawn into a shy smile beneath her prominent cheekbones.

Prior to the certificate presentation, Mother shared a few memories. As reported by the *Houtexan*, the monthly magazine of the University of Texas Health Science Center in Houston, Mother recalled how, after the accident, her fellow dental students, all men, volunteered without hesitation to give blood for her transfusions and how they came to the hospital to pin her as a "sweetheart" in their fraternity, Psi Omega. It was like having 23 brothers, she said.

At the conclusion of her remarks, Mother thanked the Dental Branch for honoring her. "You usually don't get these kinds of things to happen until you're 'pushing up daisies,'" she added, sending a ripple of chuckles and applause through the audience. "I'm glad to be able to smell the flowers."

Mother tells her story for an oral history project at the University of Texas Dental Branch, May 1984

Chapter Nineteen
Knowledge is the Key

By the summer of 1982, Mother had become a grandmother three times over: to Chris, who would turn 4 in September; to Amy, born in 1980; and to newborn Jonathan, who arrived on July 29. A fourth grandchild, Robbie, would join the family at the end of 1985. All four children were born with profound, congenital hearing loss, the result of inheriting two copies of a recessive gene—one from each parent. Bob and Cindy each had one copy of the gene; their hearing was normal. But when two copies of the gene were put together, that's what caused the deafness.

This was extraordinarily difficult for my brother and sister-in-law. When the children were old enough to go to school, Bob and Cindy struggled to find places that could accommodate their disability, places where they could learn and thrive. Amy remembers "bouncing around" from school to school, her parents trying to find one place after another where she would be accepted. They tried to mainstream her in regular classes in public school, placed her in special education classrooms and in private school, and even sent her away to boarding school. The constant upheaval left its mark.

"I often acted out in the classroom, because I never knew what was going on," Amy said. "I often daydreamed, got in trouble, and couldn't focus because I missed out on the academics that were taught before the assignments. Growing up, I was often behind my peers due to lack of accommodations and accessibility."

Mother couldn't fix this situation. Without hands, she obviously couldn't communicate with sign language. But she was ever resourceful, and she was determined to find a way. When they were children, while Bob and Cindy were at work, she'd pick them up after speech therapy, take them home and cook dinner for them. Whenever Bob and Cindy needed a break, Mother would bring the children home with her, overnight, and sometimes for the weekend. "I have fond memories of her sitting at her makeup table doing her make up," Amy said, "and feeding my younger brothers from a spoon in her mouth. She couldn't feed herself, but she could feed us until we were old enough to do so."

Mother with Bob and her grandchildren, from left, Amy, Jonathan, baby Robbie, and Chris, Christmas 1986.

Mother encouraged her grandchildren to express themselves. In the summers, she enrolled them in Vacation Bible School at her church, Immanuel Baptist, and took them to the neighborhood pool to swim. "She didn't baby us. She wanted us to be with other kids and have confidence," Amy said. "Sometimes I think I get my confidence from her because she was so outspoken, but always kind."

Once, during the summer of 1988, 6-year-old Jonathan fell into the deep end of the neighborhood pool and panicked. Mother didn't hesitate. Instead of calling for help, she rushed to the side of the pool and leaned over as far as she could, trying to snag her thrashing, wailing grandson with the hook at the end of her prosthesis. Finally, a lifeguard dove in and retrieved him.

"I remember it like it was yesterday," Amy said. "She didn't wait for a lifeguard or someone else. She went straight to him to try to grasp him." No doubt others who were at that pool that day remember the scene just as vividly—a 71-year-old woman without arms trying to rescue her grandson, on her own.

When Amy lived at boarding school, she couldn't use the pay phone because of her deafness. So "Me-Ma," as Amy called her, wrote letters to her granddaughter instead while holding a pen in her mouth. She also encouraged Bob and Cindy to use oral communication—spoken speech—at home. That early training enabled the children to catch up quickly to their peers once—as teenagers—they received cochlear implants, small electronic devices that enabled them to hear the spoken word for the first time.

"My grandma played a huge role in my parents' decision to immerse us in the hearing world," Amy said. "My grandma was always brainstorming ways to help me growing up. She would discuss the issue, and what we could do to solve the problem. I always appreciated her non-judgmental and loving guidance, no matter how much trouble I was in at home or school.

"People often stared at my grandmother when we went in public, but it didn't faze her. She was used to it, and often used the opportunity to educate people about her story and how it changed her. I wear 'Kanso' off-the-ear sound processors, which look a lot different from cochlear implants. People stare when I wear my hair up. I try to use those opportunities to educate people about hearing devices. I don't get offended when people ask me odd questions. Most have never seen a Kanso implant before.

"What people don't understand isn't their fault. Knowledge is the key to make this world a more accepting place."

1982 was not such a good year for Dad, who was growing increasingly restless in his adopted country of Israel. His relationship with Paula had worn thin, largely because he could barely tolerate her sons smoking in the house during frequent visits. Paula's grandchildren were especially irritating.

"Our present child-centered civilization gives me a pain," he grumbled in a letter to me. "One can hardly be in the same house with the little spoiled monsters. And the main trouble is the parents. (Dr.) Spock has done a lot of harm. Punishment is almost non-existent. Nuts ... When I hear parents call their kids and get the answer, 'I don't want to come,' this makes me want to get a whip."

Thus, it came as little surprise to me that in 1983, 13 years after he moved to Israel, Dad announced that he was coming back to the States—alone. He decided to settle in Philadelphia, I suppose, because that's where his cousin Stella lived. I was not too far away, eight miles up the Main Line in Narberth.

Still the solicitous son, I tried to get together with him once a month or so. One time we were walking after dinner and I asked him, "How come you were never willing to get professional help?"

Dad just shrugged and said, "I had too much pride."

By 1983, I was in a serious relationship with Jacqueline. She'd been my boss when I ran the dormitory during graduate school, and we continued our friendship after I moved to Narberth. She was married at the time but later divorced, and afterwards she accepted my invitation to visit me. We started to date long distance, back and forth between Massachusetts and Pennsylvania, and in early 1984, we decided that I'd move back to Massachusetts, and we'd get married. About that time, Jacqueline and I visited Dad in Philadelphia, but he was not particularly warm toward her. As a result, we did not invite him to our wedding.

Jacqueline was the head of a large boarding high school just south of the New Hampshire line. We lived on the grounds of the school in a house we shared with her two children from a previous marriage, aged 11 and 14. I worked for a substance abuse hospital in Spofford, NH, for four years and then went into private practice in Keene, about 10 miles to the east.

In 1986, at the age of 69, Mother retired from the full-time faculty at Meharry, although she would continue with part-time duties for another three years. Betty Weitemeyer continued to care for her mornings and evenings, as she had for the past 10 years, even after her husband George died after a lengthy illness in January 1987. But by the end of that year, as Mother put it, "finally the Lord laid it on her that I would be taken care of, and she left to go to a retirement center in Michigan."

Mother did not know how she was going to manage. But once again, she leaned on her faith.

Help eventually came in the form of another neighbor, Georgia Angeline Prenzel Wallace, who lived around the corner on Central Avenue, and who had many times offered to help Mother.

Novelist R.O. Kwon has described the state of deep grief as a feeling that the world has "cracked open" and fallen apart. That's what I experienced in 1990, when my marriage crumbled beneath my feet. I became profoundly depressed. I contacted a psychiatrist I knew in Keene, where I had my practice. He prescribed an antidepressant. I moved out of our marital home, stayed briefly with a dear friend, found a one-bedroom apartment in Keene, and relied on old friends for support. As I worked diligently with my therapist, I realized that I needed to escape the loneliness of single life in small-town New England. In 1991, I decided to move to a larger city where I could build a new practice, a new community, and a new life. The cities I knew best were Boston, Philadelphia, and Honolulu, where as a college sophomore I'd spent a pivotal summer.

And, of course, Nashville.

Nashville, frankly, was not high on my list. I had lived in the Northeast for 25 years. I thought I had changed so much I could never again be happy living in the South. I couldn't imagine that I would not find the intellectual environment in my hometown stultifying, the religious climate oppressive. Moreover, as I entered my 40s, I did not think I would be able to develop the quality and depth of close friendships, particularly with men, that had sustained me during my years in New England and Philadelphia.

I've always been an organized person. My friends marvel at how I file everything away at home neatly in its own place so that when I wish to reacquaint myself with a paper or document or reminiscence dating back decades, I can lay my hands on it at a moment's notice. My search for a new home was conducted in the same way: I was organized, intentional and deliberate. I did a pro/con list for each of the cities under consideration and assigned points for climate, religious environment, and the ability to start a new practice. To my surprise, when I added up all the points, Nashville came out on top.

Dad was still in Philadelphia at the time. But he was becoming increasingly depressed, living alone. Bob and I convinced him to move closer to family. He eventually agreed and asked if he could stay with Bob and his family in Gallatin.

This seemed out of character for Dad, who had long expressed disdain for Bob's family, at least to me. He was his usually disagreeable self when Cindy first met him in 1984 on the way to attend my wedding. But Bob was always solicitous when it came to Dad. Like me, Bob followed a script, and his was to win his father's favor. I don't know if Dad was invited or whether he invited himself, but over the years, he had visited Bob and Cindy on several occasions during holidays, including Christmas. Because he was Jewish, they weren't to talk about Jesus when he was around.

That summer, in 1991, Bob and I moved Dad to the two-bedroom, one-bathroom house Bob and Cindy shared with their four children, aged 12, 11, 9, and 6. "We made him a room on the back porch," Cindy recalled. Even after the move, Dad was still significantly depressed. "He stayed in bed the whole time," she said. "We kind of ignored him."

Bob and Cindy

"I wasn't very close to my grandfather," Amy added. "He was always upset about something. We were too loud or made too much noise. I think his expectations were too high for us to meet. He was always complaining about something ... I never felt connected to him, like I did with my grandma."

During the hard years, when Bob struggled with alcohol and drugs, "my grandma always made sure to try to keep our lives normal. She was very honest about my dad's issues. Yet she was a calm presence during this difficult time. It was easy to sit down and talk with her.

"I believe having a grandma like my Me-Ma shaped me into the advocate I am today," Amy said. "My son has autism, and it's a challenging journey. I've learned that I have to speak up at meetings and brainstorm solutions to help my son, just like my grandmother taught me as a child. I started a Facebook page to help local families. We discuss many issues, from therapies to medications. I also foster kids with special needs. I advocate for these kids so they can get the services and therapies they need.

"Imagine having non-verbal children with no way of communicating. When you set them up in speech therapy, or with an augmentative and alternative communication (AAC) device, you are forever changing their lives. Their difficult behaviors can decrease, and their quality of life can increase when they are given a way to communicate.

"My grandmother taught me that everybody is different. Everybody has a purpose," Amy said. "Everyone should help each other and be kind to each other always."

Amy and her daughter Becca, Christmas 2000

Chapter Twenty
A Path with Heart

In his classic work, *The Hero with a Thousand Faces*, mythologist Joseph Campbell describes his theory of the archetypal hero who answers the "call to adventure" and, while traveling "the road of trials," is transformed into something entirely new.

The heroic figure in my life will always be my mother. Nor would I ever call the end of my first marriage an adventure. It was more like a helpless slide into despair. Yet there are heroic aspects to the Buddhist path I've chosen. Like Campbell's hero, I view my life as an intentional journey, a practice. Walking my life path requires diligence and humility. For no matter how gracefully I try to walk, there is always a rough spot up ahead, the rock that strikes my foot.

As one of my teachers at Naropa, Jack Kornfield, put it in his remarkable book, *A Path with Heart: A Guide through the Perils and Promises of Spiritual Life*, the inevitable difficulties of life can, for one who is spiritually informed, be the source of an awakening, and of deepening wisdom, patience, balance, and compassion.

Campbell enumerates 17 stages of the hero's journey. Eventually, his protagonist must leave everything behind and venture into the unknown. In this, the fifth stage of his journey, the hero is swallowed up into the "belly of the whale." He disappears and appears to have died.

In the Biblical account, Jonah spends three days and three nights in the belly of a "great fish" after he refuses God's commandment to go to Ninevah and prophesy that the city will be destroyed for its wickedness. Jonah eventually prays to the Lord, whereupon the Lord commands the fish to vomit the prophet back up on dry land.

I am not a believer in Old Testament miracles. But I could identify with Campbell's version of the fish story, in the sense that the end of my marriage forced me to separate from my known world and from my old self so that I could find my true self—to choose, as Campbell put it, "to be born again."

I remember Kornfield's introduction to what I call the Great Paradox of life. "The psychological task of life is to build a self," he wrote, while "the spiritual task of life is to let go of self." Both tasks continue throughout our lifetime.

In August of 1991, I started looking for work in Nashville, networking to see if I could meet other psychotherapists. Eventually, I was invited to join a group practice. By November, I'd packed up my things in New Hampshire and moved in with my mother, thinking this arrangement would be temporary. Little did I know.

I had not gone to church in 25 years. But when I moved back to Nashville, a psychologist colleague introduced me to the Unitarian Church. Unexpectedly, I found it to be a haven for other seekers such as myself. I was looking for a spiritual community that draws upon many sources of religious inspiration. As Kornfield would say, there are a hundred thousand skillful means of awakening.

After emerging from the belly of the whale, I began to see my father in a new light. In his book, *I Don't Want to Talk About It: Overcoming the Secret Legacy of Male Depression*, psychotherapist Terrence Real described people with personality disorders as impulsive, unable to regulate feelings, having poor judgment and showing little insight. They tend to blame the world for their problems, Real wrote, and are all, in one way or another, antisocial.

That was my father.

In the Buddhist understanding of the nature of Mind, Attachment and Aversion are the primary sources of human suffering. I began to understand that I no longer needed to attach myself to my father's disordered personality or run away from it either. I could, for the first time in my life, simply choose to be free of it, while still caring about him as my father.

Philip Chanin in 1991

I'd intended to stay with Mother only until I could find a place of my own. But living with her turned out to be so congenial and so easy that I decided this was where I wanted to be. This was where I belonged. Of course, I took care of her. In the mornings, I helped her get dressed, and in the evenings, I helped her get ready for bed. It was what needed to be done. It was very familiar, for I'd grown up helping my mother around the house. Only now it was more of a shared enterprise. She still cooked our meals; I helped wash and put away the dishes. At breakfast every morning before I departed for work, she'd read her *Tennessean* while I read my *New York Times*. I'd feed her across the kitchen table. She'd chat about what was going on in her newspaper, and I'd chat about what was going on in mine.

We'd talk about life, and love, and about Dad, and I came to appreciate as never before the choices she'd had to make and how expertly and gracefully she'd navigated, as Bruce Richards might put it, the shoals and the channels of human relationships. We also had fun together. Our next-door neighbor, Bobby Garfinkle, needed a basketball court so his daughter, who was on the team at her high school, could practice at home. We volunteered our driveway, which was adjacent to his, to create a decent-sized court. We also hired a contractor to remodel the house so I could have a larger bedroom and Mother could have a bay window with a view, and a new kitchen.

"Margaret loved the friendliness of this neighborhood," another neighbor, Mary Stone, wrote for an issue of "This Old Nabe," a newsletter published by the Richland-West End Neighborhood Association. "Other people were the center of her life. Neighbors never hesitated to come over and take things off a high shelf or help her with her clothes. She was a marvelous cook and loved to provide food for others. Whenever you helped her, you helped yourself twice as much."

Gradually, I began to recognize what I had learned from Mother growing up. She taught me how to get along with people, how to take care of myself, but also how to make friends. She taught me the importance of maintaining friendships even when one moves away. Each Christmas, she'd send 200 cards to old friends across the country. Mother was a very organized person. She had to be. I learned a lot of my self-discipline from her. She was also such a good talker. She put people at ease. I think I learned to be a good listener by listening to her talk.

In the fall of 1991, Dennis Wholey, a TV host, and the author of several self-help books, visited Mother to interview her for a new book he was working on. Published in 1992, the book, entitled *When the Worst That Can Happen Already Has: Conquering Life's Most Difficult Times*, was a collection of inspirational stories by public and not-so-public figures including Jim Brady, who was shot in the head and permanently disabled during the attempted assassination of President Ronald Reagan in 1981. Mother's story was included in a section of the book entitled "Acceptance."

"I had hoped to work fulltime until I was 78," her story began. "My mother did. My father didn't retire until he was 85. I retired my dental license Dec. 30, 1990. I am completely retired now at 74, but I stay busy. I'm actually busier than I want to be, with church activities, the home for the indigent aged, programs for handicapped people, and social functions … I don't think of myself as elderly. I don't guess I ever will, either … (Mother) often said, 'The way to keep from getting old is to have new experiences, new ideas, and make new friends …'

"I don't like the word 'handicapped,' because I think of the handicapped as being people who are so severely disabled, they can't function at all. I've never looked for a job in my life; every job has looked for me … So, I feel I have lived almost a charmed life. I have had many honors; I never asked for any of the things that came my way. God has opened all those doors for me; I don't feel I have anything to complain about …

"I can't bathe and dress myself or comb my hair, but I do put on my makeup with the aid of a prosthesis that has a hook, and I can function at home by myself … I won't say that there aren't times now that I'd give anything to reach up and run my fingers through my hair, or feel my skin, or feel my face, but when those moments come, I concentrate on something else ... I'm so blessed ... I have a whole retinue of friends I can call and say, 'The ox is in the ditch' ... I don't have hands, but I've had a thousand hands of other people to help me ..."

"Even though my marriage did not last more than 23 years, it was a good marriage until my husband's health fell apart; we've remained good friends," she said about Dad. "I was his project for those 23 years; everything centered around making me independent. I would have never driven a car without him. I would have never had a useable prosthesis if it weren't for him. In 1953, we sold the house, he resigned from his job, and we struck out for California with two babies, and nothing but the fact that UCLA wanted me as an experimental amputee. They were the ones who fitted me with an arm that I could use comfortably ... I admire him for what he did for me, and I appreciate it tremendously."

Mother's story ended with a memory of a friend who, while putting on nail polish, asked her absent-mindedly, "Margaret, what kind of polish do you use?" Realizing what she'd just said, she quickly apologized.

"But that's a compliment!" Mother responded. "I would hate to think when my name comes to somebody's mind, the first thing the person would think was, 'she's armless.' If I haven't made any more impression than that, I've made a poor one."

Mother kept busy in her retirement years. She often hosted her grandchildren and paid Cindy's tuition so she could go back to school and earn her master's degree in education in 1994. By then, Dad had emerged from his depression and had moved into his own apartment in a Christian retirement community. His doormat, not surprisingly, was emblazoned with the words "Go Away."

But he did good work, logging thousands of volunteer hours at two local head trauma recovery programs. He designed and made adaptive rehabilitation equipment for some of the residents there. At 72, Dad was still helping people with disabilities. In the spring of 1994, he was one of 10 finalists for the Nashville area's annual Mary Catherine Strobel Award, which recognizes excellence in volunteerism. The award is named for the much beloved community activist and advocate for the homeless and poor who was murdered in 1986.

Even in our quiet West End neighborhood, we weren't immune from crime.

On February 20, 1996, we woke to find Mother's white Cadillac stolen from in front of our house. Problem was, she kept her spare prosthesis in the trunk.

"I don't care so much about the car as I do about the prosthesis," she told *Nashville Banner* reporter Charlie Appleton for a story entitled "Thief gets spare arm along with Cadillac." Not only was the artificial limb expensive to replace, costing around $4,000, she said, "but it's all the stuff you have to go through to get one fitted properly—it's a real headache.

"I have this fear of getting out somewhere and something happening to the arm I'm wearing – something breaking or something like that," Mother explained. "So, I keep a spare. If I can get to the side of the road, I figure an officer will come by eventually and help me get my spare arm put on. Right now," she chuckled heartily, "I don't guess that makes much difference. I don't have my car or my spare arm."

Eventually the car was located and the juvenile who had hot-wired it for a joy ride was arrested. Mother got her arm back, but she had to pay $51 to have the car towed.

The following spring, in a talk to a gathering of women alumni of Baylor University in San Antonio, Mother shared her own perspective about how our life paths—hers and mine—had crossed.

"In 1991, I was having problems finding somebody. And I said, 'Well, I should sell my house and find a larger house for my children out in Gallatin.' ... About two months later (Marty's) health was broken, and my sons brought him back to Middle Tennessee. My oldest son (Philip) came to help him get settled and while he was here interviewed with some psychotherapy practices ... He'd been in New England for 25 years. He said, 'Mother, I think I would like to come home.'

"It's been five years now and he's still with me ... I feel that God certainly was taking care of me in this situation ... At this point in life, I don't know what the future holds for me the rest of the way down the road. You just have to be convinced you know whose hand the future is in, who holds it for us."

In early 2000, as part of his treatment for alcoholism, Bob wrote a long history of his family. With remarkable clarity and insight, he described Dad's troubled and troubling personality, and Mother's grace and courage.

"My mom is truly amazing," he wrote. "That is the only word for her. She has an artificial arm on her right side, and I've never seen anything she can't do. She says that she got very depressed during menopause but could not figure out how to kill herself. I guess that's the only thing she hasn't figured out!

"She taught dentistry at Meharry for 20 years and at age 82, although she lost the sight of one eye, she still drives her car, gives inspirational speeches, and reaches out to people in a variety of ways. She modeled selflessness to me and the importance of getting out of oneself and involved in the lives of others."

In November 2000, Dad fell and broke a hip. He died on December 5. He was 78. A service was held that Saturday at a Gallatin church. That wouldn't have been his choice, of course, but since he hadn't voiced his preference before he died, the choice was made for him.

Mother grieved. She and Dad didn't spend a lot of time together during those latter years. Mainly they saw each other at their grandchildren's birthday parties and at holiday celebrations. They hadn't lived together in more than 30 years, but I believe the cord between them was so strong even death couldn't sever it.

I asked her if she believed she would see him again. "Yes," she answered firmly. "And Mother and Daddy." She paused for a moment, and then added, "And I will be able to hug them. I will have my arms back. I will be whole."

She looked at me, cocking her head to one side, as if she were about to ask a question but then decided not to. She knew I was not at all sure about an afterlife. But that was OK. This moment was enough. That's all we're given anyway—one moment at a time. I remember thinking, "You already are whole, Mother. You are the most complete person I have ever met." But I didn't speak it out loud.

I wish I had.

On Sunday evening, January 21, 2001, seven weeks after Dad died, I came home after a meeting with my men's group to find Mother seated in her chaise lounge, in front of the TV. She smiled and said, "I'm watching a good Western."

I went to my bedroom in the back of the house. About 40 minutes later I heard sounds of distress coming from her bedroom. I rushed back. Mother was having trouble breathing.

"I need to go to the emergency room," she said, her voice raspy.

"I can drive you," I offered.

"No," she said. "The ambulance will have oxygen."

She asked me to help her to the toilet. Before I could call 911, she closed her eyes, and she was gone. She died in my arms.

For the second time in a decade, my world cracked open. But this time I did not fall into a chasm of depression. Yes, I missed her horribly. After 20 years, I still miss her every day. But I was at peace. She was where she wanted to be.

Home.

Mother died just 47 days after my father. She was 83. It wasn't so much that she wanted to be with him.

Rather, I think, she knew her job was done.

Epilogue
Love People, and Feed Them

The memorial service for Margaret Jones Chanin was held in the vaulted-ceiling sanctuary of Immanuel Baptist Church in Nashville, her religious home for nearly 37 years. On the morning of January 27, 2001, sunlight streamed through the 24-foot-high faceted glass window above and behind the baptistry. Designed and constructed in Chartres, France, the window shimmered with all the colors of the rainbow and with the subdued outline of a resurrection cross in its center.

Hers was a simple service. A longtime friend, singer, and motivational speaker, Jana Stanfield, sang "Amazing Grace" and the popular Bobby Womack song, "That's The Way I Feel About You," accompanied on the guitar by Jerry Kimbrough.

Bob, Cindy, their children, and I were seated in the first row. Afterwards, Bob got up first and went to the pulpit to deliver his eulogy. Of Mother, he said, "She journeyed through life with a poise and grace, which I have never observed in any other human being.

"When I was 15 years old, I had my first epileptic seizure. During my stay at Vanderbilt Hospital, my neurologist came into my room and began to tell me all the things I could never do. Naturally, as a teenager looking forward to life, I was devastated. After he left, my mother came in, looked me in the eye and said, 'Bob, you can do anything you want to do!' It never occurred to me to doubt her as she had demonstrated that principle throughout her life. She never thought in terms of whether she could or could not do a particular thing. She figured out how to do what she wanted to do, and most important, she never hesitated to ask for help. She had discovered that amazing truth that people want and need to help others; they just need the opportunity.

"Many of you know that I have struggled with addiction for the last few years. During this painful time, my mom, my dear wife Cindy, and my brother have not given up. They prayed for me, encouraged me, and continued to love me unconditionally. I am so grateful to God that Mom saw me, not only clean and sober, but working an AA program and seeing it as God's provision for my recovery.

"I share this because Mom never loved anyone because of who they were or what they had accomplished. She saw everyone as created in the image of God and treated them with dignity and respect. Her humility came from that wonderful sense of powerlessness that enables one to connect with the One who is all power. The Apostle Paul said it best: 'When I am weak, then I am strong.' My mother's so-called handicap enabled God to use her. Our independence is our handicap. Her handicap made her useful and useable.

"Finally, many would listen to her constructive criticism, when they would receive advice from no one else. She could praise the good, point out the bad, and offer a solution with true genius. We always knew she loved us and that she really cared."

At that moment, overcome with emotion, Bob pulled a handkerchief from the pocket of his trousers and pressed it over his eyes. Cindy went up to him, put her arm around him, and helped him to his seat. Then she returned to the pulpit.

"Mothers-in-law are often the brunt of jokes, but I can't relate to that at all," she began. "Mine was wonderful. First of all, she was an excellent role model, especially of homemaking and hospitality. Even if guests just dropped by, she made them feel so welcome. Relationships were important to her, and she took time to have them and maintain them. Drop-in guests would usually end up at the kitchen table with a snack. She was a great listener and conversationalist. She really knew how to draw people out. If she happened to be busy, she'd tell you, so that you knew she didn't do things out of duty or obligation but because she wanted to.

"She was a great cook. She planned ahead; so she was never stressed or frazzled. Phil once had a house concert and 21 friends, and Margaret cooked all the entrees. She really knew how to create an ambiance. The table was always beautiful, but again the most special part was the feeling that she was so glad to have you and the great conversation that ensued. She didn't have ego needs that were unmet, so she was able to focus on others.

"She offered support and encouragement but did not offer unsolicited advice. She never interfered and she went the second and third mile helping us in any way she could, whether it was babysitting, sending a meal home, or getting us out of a financial jam. She was one of the most generous people I've ever met. She didn't have a sense that what belonged to her was hers; instead, it was ours, and she was glad to help. She gave as much as she could, instead of as little. She has also passed that trait on to her sons. I hope that one day I can be that way, too."

Then it was 17-year-old Jonathan's turn. Jonathan, the third of Mother's four grandchildren, began by recounting her story, how her fiancé had been electrocuted in the horrible accident that also took her arms, how—with the support of her family and at the urging of the dean of the Dental College—she returned to school and how, when she graduated, Dean Elliott had hung her diploma around her neck.

"This moment was captured on film and shown in movie venues around the country," Jonathan said. "Rejuvenated by her story, disabled war veterans wrote to say how the clip had inspired them ... The world's only armless dentist retired from medical service in 1989 having risen to the rank of associate professor of preventive dentistry and community health.

"If anyone was curious enough to want to see how this professional mom managed to cook, clean, vacuum and chauffeur her sons, she would have them over to watch, not letting it be known that learning to do these things took years of practice ... In spite of devastating loss, she had a happy, fulfilling life centered on others.

"As a deaf person, I used to believe the future held only limited possibilities and that my life could never really be fulfilled. Because of my grandmother, I now think otherwise ... My grandmother could have easily given up. It was fortunate then that she did not—for herself and for everyone in her life."

Finally, it was my turn to try to summon the meaning of my mother's life.

"Many patients come to psychotherapy with difficulties around assertiveness and self-esteem," I began. "They often don't know their own feelings, and fear speaking out loud their wants and needs. To such patients I may say, 'A goal of therapy is to be unselfconsciously in the world.' My mother, without arms, was unselfconsciously in the world. I've heard her remark, 'Our family hasn't really had any tragedies.' After she lost her arms, her own mother had often encouraged her, saying, 'God has a purpose for you.' My mother was busy the rest of her life finding and fulfilling that purpose.

"We know how often people with profound deficits will compensate by developing other strengths, as for example the blind person who develops exquisite hearing. My mother compensated for the loss of her arms in many ways. She compensated through connecting with others in a deep and caring way. She also developed an extraordinary memory for events and conversations of her loved one's lives. Recently she was retelling the story of our getting pulled over by a Maryland highway patrolman when I was maybe 8 years old. She remembered that all four of us were singing and as a result my father was unaware of how fast he was driving. And she remembered what song we were singing. Often when she'd have trouble sleeping, she'd create memory exercises, such as naming each of the 38 addresses where she'd lived in her life, and even going over the placement of the furniture in each room of each house.

"One of my spiritual mentors, Jack Kornfield, has said that the essence of the spiritual life can be stated in five words, 'Love people, and feed them.' My mother loved to cook, and she loved to provide food for others. She was a wonderful cook, and I grew up enjoying helping her in the kitchen. She'd sometimes joke about some of her friends—you know who you are—who needed to follow a recipe. Invariably, after she'd made a big pot of soup and put into it whatever was on hand, she would smile and say, 'I could never make that again!'

"Other people were at the center of my mother's life. She taught me so much about building and maintaining friendships. I learned by watching her example. Rare was the day when I'd return home from work in the evening and not find on my desk several birthday or get-well cards to friends or family, with notes she'd written with a pen in her mouth, waiting for me to add the stamps and return address labels.

"This week, turning through my mother's address book to find the names of people I wanted to be sure to notify about her death and this service, I was surprised to find the names and phone numbers of so many of my friends written there. I thought about how my friends would often tell me about long conversations they had with my mother when they had called to speak with me, and I wasn't home. They'd tell me things they learned about her thoughts and feelings that she hadn't shared with me."

I paused, and looked around the sanctuary, rebuilt in 1969 to accommodate 860 people. I marveled. On this day, nearly every pew was filled. Mother touched so many people. So many people loved her.

"I have fond memories of my high school years here, in the Immanuel Baptist Church, which was the focus of my religious as well as my social life," I began again. "In subsequent years, my mother was remarkably open to my own spiritual journey. I now have a small altar in my bedroom, which I use for meditation. Several years ago, mindful of the Bible's admonitions against graven images, I asked my mother if she'd mind my getting a small Buddhist statue for my altar. 'It's your room,' she responded, 'of course I won't mind,' seemingly surprised that I thought I needed to ask.

"There is a Tibetan Buddhist practice called Tonglen. It involves taking in the suffering and pain of others, and giving back your happiness, wellbeing, and peace of mind. In Tonglen, one breathes in another's hurt, anger, bitterness, fear, frustration, guilt, and doubt, and breathes back compassion, calmness, clarity, and joy. One can also do this with prayer. For example, one might pray, 'May I be able to take on the suffering of others; may I be able to give my wellbeing and happiness to them.'

"This is also a way of describing what happens in psychotherapy. As a therapist, I sit with my patient's suffering and despair. I try to listen without becoming reactive or defensive or judgmental. I know that for my patient, verbalizing his or her distress and being quietly listened to is healing. I may simply reflect back verbally what I hear, which can be validating to him or her. I may help my patient try to see the unfolding story in his or her life, which may be multi-generational. As Isak Dinesen has written "All sorrows can be borne if you put them into a story." Above all I try to convey to my patient, in my words and my presence, the healing power of compassion. My presence may well be more important than my words.

"In much the same way, being around my mother was therapeutic. At the age of 24 she had endured the terrible cosmic injustice of losing her arms and the man she probably would have married in the accident. Determined not to become bitter, she struggled to rebuild her career and her life. Thus, she was deeply acquainted with suffering. So, she didn't flinch in the face of others' distress or despair. Hers was a lifelong Tonglen practice. She calmly and lovingly listened to us, conveying her interest and concern, and offered back to us, with great compassion, from her store of wisdom.

"As a psychotherapist, I understand the 'self' to be that in us which is constructed, beginning at birth, from the thousands of positive and negative interactional experiences throughout our lives. Psychotherapy is about shifting that internal balance of positive and negative experiences. And again, this same framework could describe my mother's impact on us who are here today. As psychiatrist Peter Kramer has written, 'We can all use additional self.' My mother's life was about building more self in others through her warmth and compassion. Her impact on our lives will continue long into the future."

I concluded by quoting Mary Katharine Morn, minister of the Unitarian Universalist Church, which I then attended.

"'Our ability to feel loss means that genuine love is still present,' Morn has said. 'Our ability to remember makes this possible. Remembering does not have to be living in the past. In fact, remembering can be a valuable spiritual discipline. It can remind us of who we are, where we come from, whom we have loved, who has loved us. Connecting with the forces in our lives that have shaped us can give us strength.'"

Three weeks after Mother's death, I met the woman who would become my wife. We live in the beautifully renovated home that my parents bought in 1967. I have seen good therapists for my own personal psychotherapy, and I have made deep friendships. I have built a thriving private practice, five minutes from my house. I enjoy my involvement on the faculty of the Department of Psychiatry at the Vanderbilt University Medical Center, where I work with the psychiatric residents. I mentor many young Nashville psychotherapists and assist them in building their own private practices. I particularly enjoy my work as a marital and group therapist. Each week, I lead a women's group, a men's group, and a group for the Vanderbilt psychiatric residents.

In 2017, my brother Bob died at the age of 67 after a long battle with prostate cancer. He was a good man, a good family man. He struggled, like all of us do, yet he never gave up, never gave in. I miss him every day, just as I miss my mother.

Ever since Mother passed away, I have intended to write her story.

Now, more than 20 years later, I have completed my task.

Twenty years is a long time, and yet her life is more relevant than ever. Great strides have been made in the march toward equal rights and opportunity. Yet violence and disease still claim the lives of too many Black Americans. Too many of our brothers and sisters are shunned and despised because they are "different." And too many people with disabilities, especially those of limited financial means, still lead lives of quiet—some would say muffled—desperation.

Margaret Chanin did not solve any of these problems in her lifetime. My mother was not a fixer. But she was a doer. Faced at a young age with a most extreme experience of trauma and loss, she could easily have given up and crawled into a hole to die. Instead, buoyed by her abiding faith and by the love of those around her, she confronted her limitations and overcame them.

In always reaching forth, Mother was an inspiration not only to those who knew and loved her, but also to hundreds if not thousands of others who read about her from afar. Her calm and steady demeanor, her elegant yet accessible manner, and her friendly repartee drew people to her. They were bathed in her positivity, warmed by her light. Says our friend Bruce Richards, "Margaret made us all better."

The problems of our planet can seem remote and insurmountable. We all have burdens enough of our own. Yet we can be part of the solution, too. Each of us has the power to help right wrongs, to improve the lot of others, to make the world a better place. That, I believe, is Mother's most profound and enduring gift: she led by example.

As I have gotten older, I have come to realize how Mother's path, and mine, intertwined, and how, after enduring my own suffering, I chose to emerge from the depths of despair and go on living—just as she did.

I call her "Mother of Courage," because in her quiet, calm way, she exuded the hero's endurance, fearlessness, and grit.

I cannot hope to equal that. But I try every day.

Acknowledgments

We'd like to thank everyone who helped us tell Margaret Chanin's story:

Family members Cindy, Amy, and Jonathan Chanin, and Margo Thorning; friends and neighbors Bruce Richards, MD, and Keith Weitemeyer; former students Morgan Hines, DDS, John E. Maupin Jr., DDS, MBA, and Rueben C. Warren, DDS, MPH, DrPH, MDIV; Edwin Hines, DDS, MSD, of Meharry Medical College; and Cynthia Dusel-Bacon.

Julia Drew Rather, MLS, Reference Librarian, and Sandra Parham, MLIS, Library Executive Director, Meharry Medical College Library, for their assistance with research and in granting us permission to reprint the photograph of Eugenia Mobley, DDS, MPH.

Thanks also to the following individuals and organizations for granting us permission to reprint previously published or broadcast material:

The Osceola Times, for excerpts from stories published in the newspaper between 1941 and 1969, and for the book's cover photo, which was published on February 23, 1956.

Dennis Wholey. for excerpts from his book, *When the Worst that Can Happen Already Has: Conquering Life's Most Difficult Times*, published in 1992.

George S. Curtis Sr., of Middleton, Idaho, for photos of Margaret Chanin and her sons taken by his father, Wilbur M. Curtis, and published in *the Memphis Press-Scimitar* on January 19, 1957.

Sharlot Vay Householter, of Plano, Texas, for an excerpt from "A Triumph Over Fate," written by her grandmother, Louise Berthold, and published in the April 1943 issue of *She* magazine.

The Texas Collection & University Archives at Baylor University, for excerpts from stories published in the *Baylor Lariat* October 1 and October 29, 1943, and from "Memories of a Favorite Teacher," by Gretchen P. Thomas, published in the December 1972 issue of the *Baylor Line*. Also, Baylor University radio station KWBU, for excerpts from a July 1944 broadcast.

Dr. Tiffany Greer Hamilton, associate pastor, First Baptist Church of Clemson, for an excerpt from the February 23, 1960, issue of the church newsletter, "The Tie."

Susan Sommer, editor of *Alaska* magazine, for an excerpt from Cynthia Dusel-Bacon's account of being attacked by a bear, published in the February 1979 issue of the magazine.

Elise McMillan, for an excerpt from a story she wrote entitled "Dentistry Teacher Lost Her Arms but Kept Her Dream," published in the *Nashville Banner* on June 11,1979.

The late Charlie Appleton, for an excerpt from a story he wrote entitled "Thief Gets Spare Arm Along with Cadillac," published in the *Nashville Banner* on February 22, 1996.

Mary O. Stone, for an excerpt from the Richland-West End Neighborhood Association newsletter, "This Old Nabe."

Jack Kornfield, for excerpts from his book, *A Path with Heart: A Guide Through the Perils and Promises of Spiritual Life*, published by Bantam Books, 1993.

Excerpts reprinted with permission, as follows:

Excerpts from "Kenneth Alexander Easlick 1893-1979," by D.F. Striffler, *Journal of Public Health Dentistry,* 40(1)1980. Permission conveyed through Copyright Clearance Center, Inc.

Excerpts from *Decision* magazine, August-September 1981; ©1981 Billy Graham Evangelistic Association; used by permission, all rights reserved.

Excerpt from "Loss of Both Arms Fails to Halt La Puente Housewife," published on July 20, 1955, used with permission of the *San Gabriel Valley Tribune.*

Excerpts from "Story of Courage Comes to Light," published in the *Evansville Press* on February 16,1956, © Gordon "Bish" Thompson – USA TODAY NETWORK.

Excerpt from "Professional Education—A Nine-Year Report," by Miles H. Anderson, EdD, published in the *Orthopedic & Prosthetic Appliance Journal,* June 1961; used with permission of the American Orthotic and Prosthetic Association

Excerpts from speeches given by Dr. Martin Luther King Jr. in Nashville in 1960 and 1967, reprinted by arrangement with The Heirs to the Estate of Martin Luther King Jr., c/o Writers House as agent for the proprietor, New

York, NY. Copyright © 1967 by Dr. Martin Luther King, Jr. Renewed © 1995 by Coretta Scott King.

Excerpts from "Murrey Ace, West Wins," and "Shapiro: We Were Lucky," published in *The Tennessean* on January 15, 1966, and March 9, 1966, respectively; © Jimmy Davy – USA TODAY NETWORK.

Excerpts from "Loss of arms inconvenient—but not incapacitating," published in *The Tennessean* on April 27,1967; © Judy Thurman – USA TODAY NETWORK.

Excerpts from "Life of Service Continues Despite Delay by Accident," published in *The Commercial Appeal* on May 22, 1968; © Ida Clemons – USA TODAY NETWORK.

Excerpt from "Teachers Rip A&I 'Ethics' in Firings," published in *The Tennessean* on July 16, 1968; © Jack Davis – USA TODAY NETWORK.

Excerpt from "Armless Dentist is Honored as 'Woman of the Year,'" published September 28, 1970, in the *ADA News*. Copyright © 1970 American Dental Association. All rights reserved. Reprinted with permission.

Excerpts from "New Dean Looks to Education, Care," published in *The Tennessean* on March 26, 1978; © Candy McCampbell – USA TODAY NETWORK.

www.ingramcontent.com/pod-product-compliance
Lightning Source LLC
LaVergne TN
LVHW020606200925
821560LV00041B/890